Perfect Your Exit Strategy

7 Steps to Maximum Value

Thomas Metz

Bettencourt

Bettencourt Publishing Ltd.

Part IV. The Sale Process

18 Overview of the Sale Process   83

19 Confidentiality   89

20 Negotiating the Deal   91

21 Letter of Intent   95

22 Transaction Structures   97

23 Earnouts   101

24 Understanding Due Diligence   103

25 The Purchase Agreement   107

26 Tax Planning   109

27 The Right Attorney and Accountant   111

28 Using an Intermediary   113

Afterword   119

Appendix A: Traditional Valuation Methods   121

Appendix B: Eight M&A Myths   125

Appendix C: Selecting an Investment Banker   131

Appendix D: Optimum Price and Market Timing   135

Appendix E: Due Diligence Checklist   139

About the Author   143

Index   145

PREFACE

The goal of this book is to help entrepreneurs, CEOs and business owners develop a sound exit strategy for the eventual sale of their company.

Having worked with entrepreneurs for four decades, I have tremendous respect for these men and women. Entrepreneurs take risks and entrepreneurs create value. They risk their own capital and sometimes investors' capital. Many times they fail. But it is through failure that they learn and try again. We owe a lot to entrepreneurs. If you think about it, every job in America is created by or paid for by an entrepreneur.

Anyone can be an entrepreneur. It doesn't take a college degree. It simply takes guts and determination. It takes a willingness to fail—not that entrepreneurs ever think they will fail—but it is always a possibility. I am privileged to have worked with so many courageous entrepreneurs over the years.

This book is a precursor to my book entitled *Selling the Intangible Company: How to Negotiate and Capture the Value of a Growth Firm* (John Wiley & Sons, 2009). That book describes the process of selling a company in which the value is strategic or intangible. For many technology and service companies, the value of their strategic assets is greater than the financial value that is based on earnings. That book goes into more detail and includes 50 examples and cases regarding the process of selling a company with strategic value.

My perspective is that of a boutique investment banker who has been selling technology, software and service companies for 30 years. Over that time period and many transactions later, I have learned quite a few lessons. My intent is to help entrepreneurs, CEOs and business owners benefit from this experience.

OVERVIEW OF THE BOOK

The book is divided into four parts. The first part discusses the subject of thinking about an eventual exit. Part II delves into the seven steps that will create the maximum value. Part III examines potential problems as well as the top 10 seller mistakes. Part IV is an overview of the process for selling a company.

In Part I, we begin by examining some simple questions: why do owners sell their businesses? What is an exit strategy? Why does a firm need an exit strategy? What are the benefits of preparing early? How should you make the decision to sell? What is the right time to sell? How should you think about value? Who are the ideal buyers and how will they value your company?

In Part II we illustrate seven steps that companies can take to ensure that they receive the maximum value when the time comes to sell. Some steps are obvious, like increasing revenues; some steps are not so obvious, like reducing risks. Improving a company's systems and procedures will make a company a more attractive acquisition candidate. Being ready for an unsolicited offer will help any company operate competently and effectively.

In Part III we take a look at the potential problems that can crop up during the sale of a company. There really is no end to the list of issues that can cause problems; but it's good to be aware of the general types of problems and how to head them off. We analyze the top 10 seller mistakes which are all too common. And finally we address the question—why companies do not sell. Not every sale of company process is successful and it is instructive to understand the reasons why.

In Part IV we discuss confidentiality, the letter of intent, transaction structures and earnouts. Negotiations are a critical aspect of every transaction and we review several issues involved with negotiations. Due diligence is a topic that many people misunderstand so we address that subject. It is important to hire the right attorney and accountant; we also examine the benefits of using an intermediary to assist with the transaction. Appendix A presents an overview of the three traditional valuation methodologies to help you understand how financial value is determined. Appendix B discusses eight M&A myths. We present ideas on the best way to select an advisor or investment banker in Appendix C. Appendix D explains how the optimum price is connected to market movement. Finally, in Appendix E we present a sample due diligence checklist to give you an idea about the complexity of the diligence process.

Almost all of the companies that I have sold over the last 30 years have been companies with strategic value. Strategic value is different than the financial value. With strategic value, the price depends solely on what a buyer is willing to pay. With financial value one can reference comparable transactions and industry data to support a particular valuation. The negotiating dynamic is different for strategic transactions because there is no financial rationale for an objective valuation.

Many of the ideas presented in the book relate to companies that have strategic value, typically in the technology, software and service industries. Most of the themes will apply, however, to companies in other industries. Even a company whose value is solely financial will find many of the topics constructive.

Hopefully, this book will help entrepreneurs, CEOs and owners prepare intelligently, avoid red flags and steer clear of problem areas. Business owners can improve the odds of concluding a successful transaction at a top price by being well prepared.

For more information about the author and the boutique investment bank T.V. Metz and Co., LLC, please see the website www.tvmetz.com.

Other books by Thomas Metz

Selling the Intangible Company—How to Negotiate and Capture the Value of a Growth Firm (John Wiley & Sons, 2009)

Part I. Thinking about an Exit

1 AN EXIT STRATEGY PRIMER

An exit strategy is a plan that prepares a company for the multitude of activities that are involved in the sale of a company. An effective strategy ensures that the company is organized and ready. Selling a company is a more complicated and challenging process than many owners realize; the task of can require six months to 12 months to complete.

A sound exit strategy improves the probability of a successful exit and of obtaining the maximum price when you do decide to sell. Your goal is to maximize your after-tax dollars and an intelligent exit strategy helps you achieve that objective. In addition, the well-prepared company will experience fewer disruptions and less upheaval along the way.

The prepared company is not scrambling at the last minute to get the financials in order, locate employment agreements, draft minutes from board meetings, etc. The exit strategy also involves reducing your risks and perceiving the movement in the markets.

THE COMPONENTS OF AN EXIT STRATEGY

Seven essential steps make up the components of a sound exit strategy. Companies that take these actions will ensure that they receive the maximum value when the time comes to sell. The seven steps are:

1. Assess your company
2. Sharpen your financials
3. Get your house in order
4. Improve your value
5. Reduce your risks and weakness
6. View your markets strategically
7. Be prepared for an unsolicited offer

Accomplishing these steps will help a company increase its value. Certainly boosting revenues and profits will increase value. That's an obvious one. Reducing the risks for a buyer also increases the value. There are some more mundane aspects that enhance value such as improving your processes and procedures and making sure the financial statements are accurate and current. Unsolicited offers are increasingly common and a company should know how to respond appropriately if it receives serious interest to acquire the company.

Internal and External Components

An exit strategy has both internal and external components. The internal component includes things that are inside the company, such as having good records, accurate financial statements, sound administrative practices, well-documented operating procedures, etc. A key internal component is having a strong management team with the right people in the right jobs.

The external component is concerned with things outside of the company. It includes understanding not just the current market situation, but movement in the market and viewing your market strategically. It is important to think down the road about who the most likely acquirers might be. Think beyond the predictable buyers and give some thought to adjacent market sectors where other buyers, perhaps nonobvious buyers, might reside. Acquiring your firm may be a good way for them to enter your market.

Viewing your markets strategically is the primary external component of an exit strategy and we discuss this topic in depth in Chapter 13.

GET MOVING

The importance of early preparation cannot be overstated. Business owners should begin thinking about their exit strategies two to four years ahead of time. Many owners wait until the last minute or they do not prepare at all. By then, they will be too far down the road in the sale process to effect any meaningful changes that will impact value.

Fewer than half of companies that eventually plan to sell take actions to prepare for the event. Day-to-day operations can consume a CEO or business owner. They are so busy running their companies that they do not make time to plan for an exit. This book will help them to understand what actions they need to take ahead of time to prepare for an eventual sale.

I have seen too many situations in which a company is seeking to sell and it is having difficulty responding to information requests by the buyer. They have trouble producing schedules, getting recent financials prepared, finding copies of contracts, and so on. The problem is not that the company will not eventually get these activities completed, the problem is that it presents a bad image to the buyer. The company looks disorganized; it certainly is not a well-oiled machine. Buyers lose confidence in the company. This is a bad impression and it will negatively impact the price.

Review your exit strategy to ensure that it is both effective and realistic. Every company has at least some elements of its strategy that can be improved. Be proactive—get the counsel of an M&A expert who can advise you about preparing for the sale process, about your value and about the market situation.

Remember that your exit strategy is not set in stone, so don't let that deter you from at least having a basic strategy. If things change, you can always adjust your strategy. But it is important to have a plan in the first place. A company should revisit its exit strategy every year or two to fine tune the plan and keep it up to date.

Thomas Metz

2 THE BENEFITS OF A STRATEGY

A good exit strategy helps a company operate more smoothly, steer clear of potential problems and pave the way for a successful exit. The discipline associated with planning brings benefits to the company even if you do not sell in the near term. A sound strategy encourages management to view the decisions that they make today with a longer-term horizon.

The primary benefit of a sound exit strategy is to improve the price when the company does sell. A company will not leave money on the table if it improves operations and profitability; reduces the risks and views its markets strategically.

A second major advantage of developing an exit strategy is to ensure that the sale proceeds as smoothly as possible. The process of selling a company can be brutal—both time-consuming as well as disruptive. A prepared company means less disruption. People will not be scrambling at the last minute to prepare financial schedules, get employment agreements signed, track down IP licensing agreements or draft minutes from past board meetings. The sale will proceed with fewer obstacles and problems.

A third benefit of exit strategy preparation is improved alignment. Preparation gives business owners a chance to fine tune the alignment between management and the shareholders. Sometimes the alignment is fine and other times changes need to be made in the way that managers are compensated.

Preparing for an eventual exit also encourages management to consider their set of customers. They will have thought about who the firm's customers should be down the road as well as checking for high customer concentration. Improved product alignment is another benefit of crafting an exit strategy. Perhaps some products should be eliminated and some new services added.

A fourth benefit is that the firm will be ready if a buyer makes an unsolicited offer to acquire your business. You will be able to respond competently and with less disruption to the company. Chapter 14 discusses this topic in more detail.

And fifth, if you plan to raise capital in the future, potential investors will certainly inquire about your plans for an eventual exit. A clear strategy will give them assurance about realizing a return on their investment.

And finally, an additional benefit of a sound exit strategy is that business owners will have explored questions about their long-term goals and strategic alternatives. They will have given thought to the risks of not selling. They will have a better idea about which alternatives are realistic and which create the most value.

3 MAKING THE DECISION TO SELL

The decision to sell depends on a number of factors. Five major motivations drive a company's decision to sell:

- Shareholder motives
- Management motives
- Risk reduction
- Growth and traction problems
- Market timing

These five motivations to sell a company fall into two main categories—internal drivers and external drivers. Internal drivers have to do with what is going on inside the company. External drivers are concerned with the market and the needs of buyers in the market.

INTERNAL DRIVERS

The internal drivers that prompt a company to sell are based on the company's internal situation. They are not related to issues regarding the market or the outside world. The three internal drivers are shareholder motives, management motives and risk reduction.

Shareholder Motives

Shareholders include founders, individual investors, venture capital firms and occasionally employees. Each of these groups has both similar and different objectives for seeking liquidity.

The primary shareholder reason is that the shareholders desire liquidity and a return on their investment. They may have invested their money a number of years ago and decide that it is now time to get their money back. Founders may desire liquidity because they have worked for many years and they would like to pursue other challenges or retire.

Family businesses typically have different dynamics than nonfamily businesses. Family members may differ in their opinions about the firm's growth plan and there may be some intergenerational drama. The oldest son may want to use the cash to grow the business. Another offspring may want the cash to be paid out to shareholders now. This short-term versus long-term orientation can cause clashes among family members and it may be a good reason to sell. In some cases, a family will decide to sell because no family member wants to take on the top management role.

A bad reason to sell is because the shareholders or founders desire a very high price. The company will be disappointed most of the time. This type of sale is motivated by a financial objective not by the company's particular situation. In many cases, the desire to achieve a very high price is unrealistic.

Management Motives

The second reason to sell involves management. The company may have outgrown the founder's skill set. A hired CEO may be struggling to build the company. Personality clashes may exist within the management team. There may be conflicts between management and shareholders about the company's direction and strategy.

Unfortunately, health problems, serious illness or a death can be the reason that shareholders make the decision to sell the company. Advancing age can also influence the decision to sell. In one situation that I was involved in, two brothers were managing a company that their father had founded. Unfortunately both brothers had genetic heart conditions and the stress of running the business was dangerous for them. They sold the company, even though the brothers were only in their early 50s.

Risk Reduction

Risk reduction is another reason to sell. Sometimes an entrepreneur's entire net worth is wrapped up in his or her company. The entrepreneur may have endured a high degree of financial risk for many years and now decides that less risk would be better given his or her age, financial position or concentration of net worth. In many cases, company owners take on debt to finance the growth of their businesses and they personally guarantee the debt. As the business grows, the debt often grows as well. At some point, the debt can reach an uncomfortable level for the owners. I sold one company in which the two women partners had personally guaranteed a significant amount of debt. Their motives for selling were to get out from under the burden of debt and to retire. When I successfully sold the company, the owners were relieved to no longer have the debt weighing them down.

EXTERNAL DRIVERS

The external drivers that pressure a company to sell include growth problems, market traction problems and market timing.

Growth and Market Traction Problems

The best time to sell is when the company is doing well and enjoying excellent growth and profitability. This is when the firm can sell for top dollar. Of course, few businesses want to sell when this is the case. They are enjoying the ride. Companies usually want to wait for the growth to slow before selling. In my experience, companies usually wait too long before deciding to sell.

A key reason that many companies sell is because they have reached an impasse in the market. The company cannot gain enough market traction given its current resources. The competitive situation can be a factor as well. If a business cannot keep up with the competition in developing new products and technologies, that can be a problem. Temporary setbacks are one thing but when a company has had a long period of marginal growth it might be time to sell the company.

Access to capital is another important factor. If the company has investors who are not willing to invest additional capital, this puts a damper on growth. If this is the case, it may be a good time to sell the business. Sometimes a company will sell as an alternative to raising capital. Being acquired by a larger firm with greater sales resources may be a smart move.

Market Timing Issues

Contrary to what many think, the best time to sell may not be when the company is at the top of its game or when revenues have peaked, but when the buyers desire your company the most—when the market is hot. This is when a buyer will pay top dollar.

Excellent market timing is the primary driver for receiving the optimum price when selling a company. Pay close attention to the movement in your market. Are big companies moving into your sector? Big firms move into new sectors to capture market share and to fill gaps in their product lines. If one of your competitors has been acquired by a large company, this could signal a shift in the market.

Think about the opposite situation—the market does not need these products or technology. The likely acquirers have already acquired other solutions or developed their own solutions. This is the problem when companies wait too long and it can have a negative impact on price.

No one wants to sell when things are not going well. However, if a firm waits to sell until its profits or revenues have peaked, there may be little growth left in the company. We examine how to view markets strategically in detail in Chapter 13 and Appendix D illustrates optimum price and market timing.

Why *Not* to Sell

A company should not sell if the shareholders do not need liquidity and the business is creating more value by continuing to grow. Put another way, the company should continue building when the value being created outweighs the risks of staying independent. Sometimes a business may have insufficient revenues to attract a strategic buyer; in which case, my recommendation is to continue building the business.

Summary

Timing is one of the primary reasons for getting the best price. One of the purposes of this book is to encourage business owners to think about their eventual exit several years ahead of time. What time frame is right for you—two years, four years? The optimum time may be sooner than you think. The market may be on a different time schedule than your company's growth curve.

The reason for selling is important. Buyers always want to know the reason that a company is pursuing a sale. They do not want to waste their time with a seller who is not really serious about selling or one who is simply shopping for a high price.

In the next chapter we examine the subject of value. What is a company worth? What is the right way to think about value? We explore the concepts of financial value and strategic value.

Thomas Metz

4 THINKING ABOUT VALUE

Value is the ability to generate earnings. From a market perspective, the value of a company is what a buyer is willing to pay. When selling a company, people love to quote multiples and other metrics but what really matters is what the *market* thinks. Value is solely a function of the market.

A number of factors impact the value of the company. In addition to historical earnings and potential earnings, the firm's technology, products, market position, management team and customer set will impact value. Risk also impacts the value of a company. It is important to understand the value drivers for your business.

There are two primary types of value—financial value and strategic value. Strategic value will eclipse financial value in most cases. Let us examine these types of value.

STRATEGIC AND FINANCIAL VALUE

A transaction in which the value is based on financial metrics is different than a transaction in which a buyer is acquiring strategic assets. In a financial transaction the value is based on the seller's earnings and cash flow.

A strategic transaction is one in which the value is based on the strategic fit with a particular buyer. Strategic value will vary from buyer to buyer depending on the degree to which a buyer can capitalize on the strategic assets of the selling company.

Financial Value

Financial value is value based on expected cash flows. In essence the buyer is purchasing a stream of cash flow in the future. The historical cash flows are often be a good predictor of future cash flows.

The financial value of a publicly traded company equals the stock price multiplied by the number of shares outstanding. (E.g., a company with 10 million shares outstanding and a stock price of $50 calculates to $500 million of value.) The stock price is usually highly correlated with the company's earnings. The concept is that the greater the earnings, the greater the company value. In other words, value depends on the profits.

For large privately held companies, value is a function of the company's cash flow. Depending on the growth potential and risk, cash flow multiples range between about 8 and 12 times.

What number do you use this multiple on? The answer is cash flow. How is cash flow defined? The most common definition of cash flow is earnings before interest, taxes, depreciation and amortization, commonly called EBITDA.

Most companies with revenues less than $30 million are worth between four and seven times cash flow. This metric is often used by financial buyers. You will notice that the multiple for smaller companies is not as high as that for larger companies. This is because smaller companies are riskier than large companies.

Typically, a buyer will compute the average cash flow for the last three or four years. The buyer is trying to figure out what is the *representative* cash flow. Is last year's cash flow representative? Is a four-year average more representative? Of course, the real question is what will be the cash flows in the future. Transactions are often concluded because the buyer thinks it can improve future cash flows by improving profitability.

The three traditional methods for valuing businesses are the market approach, the asset approach and the income approach. Appendix A presents a brief overview of these three methods.

People often cite revenue multiples, but these are a poor measure of financial value. They are deficient for three reasons. First, a revenue multiple does not consider the firm's profitability, market share or growth potential. These factors strongly influence the value of any business. Second, the value range is too wide to be useful. Multiples of revenue typically range between .4 times and 4.0 times. So, a company with $2.5 million in revenues is worth between $1 million and $10 million! The range is so wide that it is of no help at all. Appendix B discusses the myth of revenue multiples in more depth.

Strategic Value, a.k.a. Secret Sauce

A company with strategic value has special sauce of some kind. Strategic value depends on a buyer's opinion about the strategic assets of the company. Software and technology are the most common types of strategic value. Strategic value can also be embodied in patents, intellectual property, know-how, brand name, market position, customer relationships, development team, etc.

The value of the strategic assets depends on how a buyer will utilize those assets. Each buyer will exploit the strategic value differently. In other words, the company is worth what someone will pay for it. Value is in the eye of the beholder.

An excellent example of strategic value is a company that I sold a number of years ago. The firm, Gaard Automation, manufactured machines to polish the wafers from which semiconductor chips are created. The objective is to smoothly polish the wafers so that the surface is as flat as possible. Gaard's founder, an engineer, had invented a method to accomplish this task better than any competitor. It was truly remarkable technology. The buyer realized that this technology would give them a powerful competitive advantage and they paid a very attractive price to acquire the company.

Two aspects distinguish companies with strategic value from those with financial value. These distinguishing aspects are *invention* and *change*. A technology company invents new technologies— hardware, software and other types of technology. And by the way, technology refers to many more industries than just those in the computer or electronics industries. Companies invent technology in many other industries—chemicals, instruments, biotechnology, plastics, automobile technology and even clothing.

The second characteristic that applies to strategic value is rapid change. Rapid change refers not only to a company's technologies, but also to the rapidly changing markets that the company is participating in.

Time is often a component of strategic transactions. A buyer may want a particular technology immediately because of market conditions or competitive pressures. A company may be willing to pay a premium if it can acquire the technology *now*. If it were to develop its own technology, that might take several years and the company would miss the market opportunity. Thus, it is willing to pay a premium to acquire it now.

The term synergy has been overused in the merger and acquisition business. However, sometimes there actually are synergies. Synergies include things like cross-selling the target's products through the buyer's distribution channels, cost savings, process improvements and other benefits. These types of synergies are also considered strategic value.

For many companies, the value of their strategic assets is substantially greater than the financial value. As a result, multiples of cash flow (or EBITDA) are not applicable to companies with strategic value.

Strategic transactions are unique; therefore it is not legitimate to compare one with another. This is another reason that the multiple of revenue is an inappropriate measure. Just because one company sold for a certain multiple does not mean that another company will sell for that multiple. In addition, the value of the strategic assets is unrelated to the revenue stream. The revenues could be double or half and the key assets are still the same.

PROFESSIONAL VALUATIONS—PROS AND CONS

Is a professional valuation necessary? Oftentimes a valuation will help owners understand how a company creates value and how the value may be viewed by others.

Most professional valuations are requested to determine a company's fair market value. The definition of fair market value is the price at which a business would change hands between a willing buyer and a willing seller, neither being under any compulsion to buy or to sell, and both having reasonable knowledge of the relevant facts.

A professional valuation often determines a valuation range, not just one specific number for value. For a small company, the span from the low valuation to the high valuation can be such a wide range as not to be constructive. If operating profit is less than

$1 million, my recommendation is that the company should not spend money on a professional valuation. It is difficult to find comparable companies because the companies are private and transaction details and financial information are unknown. As a result, the valuation will be inexact and not particularly meaningful. In addition, for small companies, a minor change in expenses can have a dramatic impact on profitability. For example, if an owner were to reduce his salary then profits might double. Obviously, this does not double the value of the business.

For larger companies, with operating profits greater than $1 million, a valuation may be helpful. Using the market approach, the comparable companies are likely to be genuinely good comparables. For a strategic sale, however, a valuation is not usually relevant.

Sometimes a professional valuation can be a problem if it sets expectations too high. Putting a high price tag on a company can scare away buyers. Remember, the market is the final arbiter of value, not a professional valuation.

How will buyers view the value of your company? What do they focus on? How do buyers assess strategic value? The next chapter addresses these important questions.

Thomas Metz

5 VALUE THROUGH THE BUYER'S EYES

Companies have a variety of motives for making acquisitions. Purchasing a company can be an excellent way for a buyer to gain a foothold in a niche market, add customers and acquire new technologies and new capabilities. Before we delve into how buyers think about value, let us first explore the reasons that propel buyers to acquire other businesses.

Buyers make acquisitions for a number of reasons:

- New Products and Services—many acquisitions are made to acquire new products and services.
- New Technologies—buyers use acquisitions as a way to capture the latest technologies.
- Intellectual property—IP includes patents and technical knowledge and is becoming increasingly important.
- Market Entry—buyers use acquisitions to quickly gain footholds in niche markets.
- Gain Talent—an acquisition can provide talented people in many areas including designers, engineers and developers.
- Customers—acquiring customers is common in a consolidating market.
- Distribution Channels—acquisitions can expand a buyer's distribution channels.
- Geographic Location—buyers utilize acquisitions to expand their geographic presence.

- Gain Mass—buyers make acquisitions to add revenues and customers.
- The Price is Right—occasionally a buyer makes an acquisition because the price is too good to pass up.

How a buyer determines price depends on the degree to which the buyer can capitalize on the components of value. Buyers have different opinions of value because they have different views about the market potential, about which technologies will be successful, about which customer sectors to pursue, etc. Therefore, value will differ from buyer to buyer.

It is important to differentiate between price and value. Value is what the acquisition is worth to the buyer. Price is the amount the buyer pays. As long as the price is less than the value, the buyer should be willing to make a deal.

THE BUYER'S THOUGHT PROCESS

On a number of transactions, I have advised buyers that were looking to make acquisitions. I helped these buyers analyze how much they should pay for an acquisition. The primary question in the buyer's mind is—how can this acquisition increase the profits of our company?

Understanding the buyer's thinking process is a key part of negotiating a sale-of-company transaction. The following questions are typical of a buyer's thought process:

- What is the long-term market potential for the company? Can we grow the business significantly?
- What is the company's market share? How is the company's market specifically defined?
- What is the potential for cross-selling products?
- What are the financial projections for the remainder of this year and for next year?
- What are the real operating profits? Will increased market penetration generate incremental profitability?
- What are the components of fixed and variable costs?
- What is the profitability of each product?
- How profitable is each customer?

There are two aspects to a buyer's evaluation of value—the strategic perspective and the financial perspective. Strategic value refers to how the acquirer can incorporate the seller's business and key assets into its business. Financial value is based on the profitability and financial performance of the target.

The Strategic Perspective

The strategic perspective includes the buyer's assessment about the strategic benefits of the acquisition. Perhaps acquiring a new technology will prompt them to enter a new market sector. If the acquisition includes a new product line, the buyer may value the strategic aspects of this product line. They will examine cross-selling opportunities. The acquisition may have a competitive benefit enabling the buyer to keep up with or head off competition. Sometimes strategic value is more qualitative than quantitative.

The buyer's acquisition team will study the target in depth to figure out how the acquisition can add value to the buyer. The appropriate comparable for the buyer is how much it would cost them to develop this technology or product line on their own. For the selling company, the trick is to figure out how much strategic value the buyer sees in the acquisition.

The Financial Perspective

When the buyer evaluates value from the financial perspective, it will analyze historical cash flows and calculate value using a multiple of EBITDA. The buyer will also research the market to compare the target with similar companies and comparable sale transactions.

The buyer will use this financial value in negotiations. They will argue, for example, that since Acme Corp. sold for five times cash flow, therefore this company should also sell for five times cash flow.

The financial value has little to do with the strategic value. It is strictly used for negotiations. It is not related to how the buyer will benefit strategically from making the acquisition.

TOTAL COST OF ACQUISITION

One of the major differences between how buyers and sellers view the cost of an acquisition is the concept of *total cost of the acquisition.*

21

The seller perceives the cost simply as the price paid by the buyer. A buyer will view the cost of the acquisition as the total of every cost related to completing the transaction. These costs include the acquisition cost, legal fees, investment banking fees, integration costs, additional working capital that must be contributed, additional capital improvements and any other costs that are required to make the acquisition happen. The concept of total cost of acquisition is a good one and the buyer is smart to think in these terms.

INTEGRATED OR STAND-ALONE?

The selling company can be combined with the buyer's company in several ways. It may remain as a stand-alone company. It may become a division of the buyer. Or, it may be fully integrated into the buyer's company. The product lines could be added to the buyer's products and the seller's technology integrated into the buyer's products.

If the acquisition will remain as a stand-alone business unit, the buyer will view value more from a financial perspective. What profits will it generate in the future? There are likely to be some areas in which the acquisition will boost revenues and profits because of complementary products or services.

If the acquisition will be integrated into the buying company, the calculation for return on investment is more difficult because the acquisition's cash flow will be mingled with the parent's cash flow. Many of the overhead expenses will be shouldered by the parent company, such as insurance, accounting and legal services. The buyer will view value in terms of contribution margin. Contribution margin equals revenues minus the variable costs.

RECOGNIZING RISK

The buyer must also consider risk when determining value. It is important for the selling company to understand how a buyer views risk. A common problem is that sellers underestimate the amount of risk associated with the acquisition of their company.

Risk encompasses a number of areas: market risk, financial risk, management risk, technology risk and product risk. Each buyer will view these risks differently. For some buyers, several of these risks might not be particularly significant but another risk may be extremely important to them.

The point is that value does not exist in a vacuum but in the context of the buyer's business. Risk is the other side of the price/value coin. The better the seller comprehends its own risks, the better job it can do explaining or mitigating these risks for the buyer. Chapter 12 discusses the concept of dealing with risk in more depth.

In the next chapter we explore the various types of buyers—financial buyers, strategic buyers and the different sizes of buyers.

Thomas Metz

6 THINKING ABOUT THE BUYERS

This chapter examines the various types of buyers—strategic buyers, financial buyers, large buyers, small buyers and a few other types of buyers.

Most sellers think they have a reasonably good idea of who the likely buyers are for their company. In some situations, however, the company does not have a clear idea regarding the best buyers. Sometimes the optimal buyer is a large company in the same market. Sometimes it is a smaller company in an adjacent market that is seeking to enter the market. Occasionally, the right buyer is a company that the seller is not aware of.

TYPES OF BUYERS

The two primary types of buyers are financial buyers and strategic buyers. Financial buyers are chiefly interested in the profits and cash flow of the selling company. Strategic buyers make acquisitions in order to acquire strategic assets or achieve a strategic advantage. Most technology companies are acquired by strategic buyers. Other types of buyers include competitors, partners and occasionally, employees.

Financial Buyers

Financial buyers acquire companies to enjoy a stream of cash flows in the future. The private equity firm is the quintessential financial buyer. These investment firms are formed with the purpose of acquiring and improving businesses. In the last 20 years, private equity firms have purchased a great many companies across the United States. The price that a financial buyer pays is based on a multiple of operating earnings. Occasionally, a private equity firm will make an acquisition that complements one of their portfolio companies. Although this does have a slight strategic aspect, the price will be based on financial metrics. Of course, the best financial buyer is the one that will pay the highest price.

Strategic Buyers

Strategic buyers are focused less on financial performance and more on gaining new technologies, new products and entry into new markets. The best strategic buyer is one that can use the technology or other key assets to the highest degree. The value to a strategic buyer will almost always be greater than the value to a financial buyer. There are three types of strategic buyers:

- Obvious buyers—companies in your market sector
- Fringe buyers—companies in adjacent markets
- Emerging buyers—newer companies that have been growing rapidly

Some of the more recent acquisitions in the technology sectors involve these emerging new buyers. For example Twitter and Facebook have acquired a number of companies in the last few years. These companies have experienced rapid growth and went from being small companies to major acquirers in a short time.

SIZE OF THE BUYER

The universe of buyers can be broadly segmented into three general categories: large, midsized and small:

- Large buyers—revenues greater than $500 million
- Midsized buyers—revenues between $150 million and $500 million
- Small buyers—revenues between $15 million and $150 million

For a transaction greater than $100 million in size, the large companies are obviously the best buyers. For the sale of a company with a price between $30 million and $100 million, the most likely buyers are midsized buyers and occasionally the large companies. For a transaction that is less than $30 million the most likely buyers are the small buyers. The large buyers are rarely interested in transactions less than $30 million.

Large Buyers

One of the mistakes that I have seen over the years is that small companies believe that the largest companies are the best buyers for them. As a result, they end up focusing on the wrong companies. It is much better to focus on the midsized and smaller buyers even though these companies are not as visible.

A small acquisition will rarely make an impact on a $1 billion company. So unless your company has revenues greater than about $50 million, it is not productive to reach out to large buyers. It is simply too small to get their attention.

Midsized Buyers

An acquisition is an excellent way for a midsized company (with revenues from $150 million to $500 million) to add capabilities and expand into new markets. A midsized buyer acts a lot like a big buyer; however, the midsized buyer will consider a small acquisition of $10 million or $20 million if it achieves a strategic objective.

A typical midsized buyer will have a small team that is experienced in the acquisition process and they will likely have made acquisitions in the past.

Small Buyers

Small buyers are best for small acquisitions. A $5 million or $10 million acquisition is an important transaction for a small buyer. Many small buyers are on a rapid growth track and they will make acquisitions to spur their growth.

Small buyers are usually more difficult to discover. They are small and privately owned so they are less visible and harder to identify. One downside is that smaller buyers may not be experienced in making acquisitions.

Problem Buyers

Smaller buyers and some midsized buyers are risker buyers; and every now and then, they can become problem buyers. For example, a friend of mine sold her company for price that included a significant earnout. She had confidence that her business would continue to be profitable and that the threshold for the earnout payment would be met. However, she neglected to perform due diligence on the buyer. It turned out that when the earnout payment was due, the parent company was in dire financial straits. She and her partner were unsecured creditors and never received the money, despite a court judgement in their favor. The lesson is to know who you are dealing with. Do your homework on the buyer.

OTHER TYPES OF BUYERS

A few other types of buyers are worth mentioning. These buyers are not major acquirers but from time to time they do make acquisitions. These buyers include competitors, partners and employees.

Competitors as Buyers

Competitors are rarely the best buyers. Even if the seller's technology is superior, it is highly unlikely that the competitor will replace its current technology with the seller's technology. The buyer prefers its own technology because they know it and understand it.

Consolidation is the typical reason behind acquisitions made by competitors. Acquisitions in a consolidating industry are usually made to gain customers. These types of transactions generally do not pay high prices because the customers are the only real asset. Occasionally a competitor will utilize an acquisition to fill a gap in its product line and this is a good motivation for an acquisition.

Partners as Buyers

A company that has a partnering relationship can be a good potential buyer for a business. Obviously they know the business well and they probably have a reasonable idea of the value. Some partner companies have access to capital but often the transaction will be structured with debt owed to the sellers. Similar to

28

competitors, partners generally do not pay a very high price for acquisitions.

Employees as Buyers

Employees seldom have enough cash to purchase the business; thus, the owner or shareholders cannot cash out. In some cases, the owner will accept payments over several years. Employees generally are not risk takers; however, and assuming a debt may be beyond their comfort level.

A friend of mine had built a successful small business that was a leader in its market niche. He was getting older and it was time to retire. He had strong loyalty to his employees so he offered to sell the company to the employees for $10 million. The employees did not have enough money to make a down payment nor did they want to take on debt going forward so they declined. Two years later he sold the company for $14 million. The employees could have made an excellent gain if they had purchased the company, but it was not their risk nature to do so.

WHO ARE THE BEST BUYERS?

What types of companies make the best buyers? The answer is easy for a financial transaction—it is the buyer willing to pay the highest price with the best terms. The best strategic buyer is the one that needs the technology or products the most. They have products and services that complement, but do not overlap, those of the selling company. They will be willing to pay the highest price. These strategic buyers are often in adjacent markets and want to enter that market quickly.

Many CEOs believe that they know who the best buyers are ahead of time. This is not always the case in my experience. Many times the best buyers are not in the selling company's primary market; they are in adjacent markets. In addition, the best buyer may not be the first company that makes you an offer.

More is Better

The best situation, of course, is when there are more buyers. Multiple buyers increase the seller's bargaining power. With several buyers in the picture, it is possible to negotiate back and forth, ensuring that each buyer offers its highest price. When there is only one buyer, negotiations are a little trickier. When selling a company, one of the key roles of the investment banker is to generate multiple offers.

Now that we have an understanding of value and a familiarity with the various categories of buyers, it is time to press forward and explore the seven essential steps that can help a company to obtain the maximum price.

Part II. 7 Steps to Maximum Value

7 THE 7 STEPS

What actions can you take that will increase the value of your company when you eventually sell? How can you improve areas of weakness that might raise red flags? Every business has some areas that need improvement; however, there are measures you can take to maximize the price and avoid leaving dollars on the table.

These seven essential steps will help companies sell for the maximum price.

1. Assess Your Company

The first step is to assess your company by asking the critical questions. How will a buyer view your company? Make sure that you are defining your company in a constructive way. Are the goals of shareholders and management aligned properly?

2. Sharpen Your Financials

Financial records are a reflection of the quality and soundness of the business. Make sure that your capital structure is shipshape and properly documented. Financial issues can spoil a transaction faster than any other problem.

3. Get Your House in Order

Get your administrative and operating procedures right. Ensure that your intellectual property is well documented. Make sure that your management team is complete with the right people in the

31

right jobs. If your house is in order it will build confidence in the buyer throughout the sale process.

4. Improve Your Value

Drive up revenues and margins as much as you can. Increase the amount of recurring revenues. Reduce the working capital requirements. Manage the profitability of your products. Manage your customer mix and know the profitability of each customer. Minimize any potential liabilities.

5. Reduce Your Risk and Weaknesses

Reducing business risk will have a positive influence on value. Risky companies are not worth as much as low risk companies, even with the same level of profits. Be aware of the risks in your business and take steps to reduce these risks. Every business will have areas of weakness, but strive to minimize these concerns.

6. View Your Markets Strategically

Viewing a market strategically means perceiving where the movement is occurring in the market and recognizing the probable effects of that movement. It means understanding who the best buyers might be and why.

7. Be Prepared for an Unsolicited Offer

Unsolicited offers occur more often than you might realize. Be in a position to respond intelligently and with a realistic plan of action in case you receive an unsolicited offer.

8 ASSESS YOUR COMPANY

The first task to perfecting your exit strategy is to critically assess your company. This involves asking the right questions and being forthright with the answers. Every company should ask some good hard questions from time to time. You may not have answers for every question but the questions will be helpful in guiding your actions as you move forward building your business.

This assessment examines how you define your company, how you operate the company and how the company fits in the marketplace. Every business changes over time—sometimes only slightly and sometimes dramatically. It is also a good idea to periodically check the alignment between different groups of shareholders and between shareholders and management.

The benefit of this assessment is a better understanding of your company, its place in the market and your connection to your various customer groups. It also helps your employees to understand their mission. Clarity is critical.

Once a year every company should go through this self-assessment process. It might require a half-day session or as long as a full weekend retreat. In any case, an honest assessment will benefit the company.

Who should do the assessing? Certainly management is the primary group to assess the company. It is also advantageous to get input from outside board members and from an independent professional who can be objective.

WHAT ARE THE IMPORTANT QUESTIONS?

A business owner must ask a number of critical questions about his or her company. What are your strengths? What are you good at? What things need to be improved? What weaknesses need to be addressed? Where are you exposed? Important tasks include examining your markets and product mix, your management team, operating procedures, customers and competitors.

The preceding questions are internally focused questions. It is important to ask some externally focused questions as well. Two of the most important external questions are: how might a buyer regard your company? And, how might a buyer view your value? The answers to these questions can be very enlightening to business owners.

Let us take a more in-depth look at these important questions.

Market Questions

First of all, think about your markets:

- What markets are you participating in?
- How would you define your market?
- What market sectors should you address that you are not in now?

Customer Questions

Ask yourself the pertinent questions about your customers:

- What problem do you solve for you customers?
- What types of companies are your customers? What is the common thread between the companies that are your customers?
- What makes one company or customer a better candidate for your products than another company?
- List your top 15 customers. What is the revenue per customer?
- Should you fire any of your customers?

Competition Questions

Some businesses do not pay as much attention to their competition as they should. Your competitors are a moving target. Your past competitors may be different from your future competitors. It pays to keep a watchful eye on your competition, particularly potential future competitors. Ask good questions about your competition:

- Who are your primary direct competitors?
- Who are your indirect competitors?
- How is your company different from your competitors?
- How do you compete effectively against them? Why do customers buy your product instead of your competitors'?
- Stated differently, if a company does not buy your product, how do they solve their problem?

Sales Process Questions

Your sales process is another area that should be examined. These are a few good questions:

- What kind of objections do you hear when making sales calls?
- What does the market think of you?
- How is your company perceived?

Systems and Procedures Questions

Sometimes administrative issues take a backseat. Establish sound systems, procedures and accounting practices. They will pay dividends when the time comes to sell the company. Your procedures could benefit from asking a few tough questions:

- Are your procedures and systems well documented? Well-documented systems create value in the mind of a buyer.
- What management processes are working well?
- What management practices should be reevaluated?
- Do you have areas in which new processes need to be put in place or improved?

Check Your Company Definition

How do you define your company? The answer to this question can have a significant impact on the way you plan for new products or enter new markets. Your company definition will impact your eventual exit. Do you even have a company definition?

- Why does your company exist?
- Why is that important?
- In what ways are you truly different?

Check Your Alignment

Alignment refers to agreement on the company's goals and the strategy for achieving those goals. There must be correct alignment between several groups. First is alignment between members of the management team—are they in synch? Second is alignment between management and the shareholders. The third type of alignment is between different groups of shareholders. Sometimes management or the owners may not realize that a conflict of interest exists between management or shareholder groups. Shareholder groups might have differing objectives; their investment horizons might be dissimilar. One group might have a short-term time horizon and another group may be more interested in the long term-plan. It is important to recognize such a conflict early on and make changes before problems come to a head.

How Will a Buyer View Your Company?

What will a buyer think your company? How will they view your product mix and customer set? How will they assess your management team? What will a buyer think about your financial statements? These buyer questions were addressed earlier in Chapters 5 and 6. We reconsider these questions here because an important part of assessing your company is understanding how a buyer will view your company.

Summary

Most businesses are imperfect. There are always things that could be done better. However, if you plan to sell your company in the next few years, it makes good sense to improve any existing problem areas. Your company may not be perfect, but it likely could be improved. The benefit of continually improving your company is greater value and a higher price.

Now that you have completed a straightforward assessment of your company, the next step is to review your capital structure and perfect your financial records.

9 SHARPEN YOUR FINANCIALS

Financial issues can derail a transaction faster than most issues. Sound financial records are critical. As part of your exit strategy preparations, it is essential to evaluate the financial statements as well as the capital structure. In addition to accuracy, a company's financial records are a reflection of the quality and soundness of the business.

GET YOUR CAPITAL STRUCTURE RIGHT

Before we discuss the financial statements, an area that tends to get short shrift is the capital structure. Getting your capital structure right is the first thing a company needs to do. Many times the capital structure is not a problem, but sometimes it can be a big problem and require months to iron out before the company can move forward with a transaction.

Are your shareholder records correct? Do you have any issues with shareholders? Is your capital structure wobbly? Multiple financing rounds with multiple shareholder groups can occasionally produce capital structure problems.

The company's shareholder records must complete and accurate. In one transaction that I was working on, the outside accountant discovered that the company had never issued 20,000 shares of stock to one of the shareholders. The company had completed several rounds of financing. In this case, one of the original shareholders had purchased additional shares in a later financing round; however, the company never issued the shares to him. The company did issue the stock and it was not a problem, but it could have been troublesome. Problems like this cast doubt on the accuracy of a company's shareholder records.

The point is that even though these seem like minor issues, it is better to resolve them earlier rather than later. It is absolutely critical to resolve all shareholder issues before the sale process begins.

GET YOUR FINANCIALS RIGHT

Reviewing the financial condition is a good exercise for every company. The company should get its accountants involved before the sale process begins. Use it as an opportunity to clean up your financial reporting and improve your internal controls.

What does it mean to have your financial statements in order? First of all, they must be accurate. They must not leave questions unanswered. They must not have ambiguous terms. Do your statements reflect the true situation? Your internal controls should be more than just passable; they should be very good.

A buyer will want to review profit and loss statements and balance sheets for the last three or four years. Make sure that your statements are complete and accurate. Problems regarding financial statements include items such as:

- Do you have any accounting conventions that are peculiar to your business? Sometimes companies have idiosyncratic ways of accounting for certain items. Identify these areas and switch to conventional accounting methods.
- Have some items been recorded and then re-categorized later? (For example, service revenues.)
- Is there difficulty comparing performance from year to year? Do the categories track from year to year? (E.g., cost of goods sold.)
- Are there any liabilities that are not stated on the balance sheet, such as accrued vacation pay? Never surprise a buyer with hidden liabilities.

Sometimes simple things can cause problems. Are the accounts receivable accurate and up to date? Are the accounts payable records complete? Is inventory current? Any obsolete inventory should not be counted as part of the current inventory. Poor financial records raise questions and doubts in the minds of buyers which is always a bad thing.

Put procedures in place so that financial statements can be prepared on a monthly, or at least quarterly, basis. If it has been nine months since the company's last official income statement, this can be a problem. It may take another month or two to prepare an interim statement. It makes a seller look bad when it cannot provide timely financial statements.

Working capital is an area that many companies do not fully understand. Working capital is defined as current assets minus current liabilities. It is usually analyzed as a percentage of revenue. If a company does not have the right amount of working capital, a buyer will view this as a liability and it reduces value. Managing your working capital effectively is a good practice. It can increase your value. We review working capital in depth in Chapter 11.

Remove any personal assets from the company's books such as vacation homes or boats. If there are any unusual shareholder loans it is a good idea to clean them up as well. Business owners, especially founders, are notorious for co-mingling personal and business transactions. Real estate should never be part of the operating company; keep it separate.

TAX ISSUES

Tax issues can be problematic. This seems simple enough but you would be surprised at how many times small issues pop up and rock the boat. Do you have any unpaid taxes? Do you have any disputes with the IRS or other taxing authorities? Make sure that the company has filed its tax returns in a timely fashion and that it has complied with all tax regulations.

Ensure that the tax returns are complete, filed and in order. If there are any significant differences between your tax returns and the financial statements, have a cogent explanation for these differences.

FINANCIAL PROJECTIONS

Projections for the profit and loss statement should be prepared for the next few years. These projections should be reasonable and achievable. Companies that project overly optimistic revenues and profits get into trouble because they appear unrealistic and if there is an earnout, they will have difficulty achieving the projections. Be sure to state the assumptions that support the financial forecast. You want to show your business in the best possible light, but you also should be absolutely truthful about every aspect of your business.

DO YOU NEED AN AUDIT?

Audited financial statements are not required for the sale of most companies. It depends on the size of the company. If the buyer is a publicly traded company or a large privately held company it will prefer audited statements. A privately held buyer that plans to go public in the near future will also require audited statements.

A small privately-held buyer will rarely require audited statements. Audited statements are generally not worth the cost. Good clean records that have been reviewed by an accounting firm should be good enough in most instances.

For small acquisitions, the transaction is often structured as a sale of assets, not a sale of stock, so an audit would not be required. If a buyer does insist on audited statements, this can be accomplished later in the process. Even though an audit may not be required, sound financial statements and sound accounting practices will add value to the company.

In summary, financial issues are less problematic and less expensive to remedy if they are addressed early on than if they are uncovered during the due diligence process. Now we turn to getting your house in order, which includes administrative practices, operations, employee matters and intellectual property.

10 GET YOUR HOUSE IN ORDER

G etting your house in order is an essential aspect of perfecting your exit strategy. This includes putting sound practices in place, cleaning up loose ends and preparing the company for eventual sale. Even if you don't plan to exit for several years, sound practices are an excellent way to operate your company— organized, focused and prepared. Performing an exit strategy review process will pay big dividends.

Get your people right. Be sure to have a complete management team. Make sure your incentives are strong and that you have employment agreements for the key people. Have a succession plan and put stay-put incentives in place before the sale process begins.

Get your operations and administrative practices right. Make sure that your policies and procedures are solid. Ensure that your corporate records are organized, legal issues are managed and that your website is current.

Get your intellectual property right. Intellectual property is becoming increasingly important in the acquisition of many companies, not just technology companies. More and more companies have intellectual property.

GET YOUR PEOPLE RIGHT

People issues are some of the most important issues regarding the acquisition of a company. This is an area where thinking down the road a year or two can be quite beneficial. Your goal should be to achieve management depth and stability. Putting a new sales manager in place, for example, can be a real plus when the time comes to sell the business.

Anticipating a potential transaction can give management the impetus to deal with personnel issues. Replacing people takes significant time and effort but it will pay off when you have a solid team in place. If there are family members on the payroll it is a good idea to evaluate the need for their employment.

Occasionally there are problem employees. There might be one or two people, although not big problems, who can still cause stress in the organization. It may not be pleasant to deal with such issues but it might be necessary. The organization will be healthier going forward if problem employees are given a chance to improve and if they don't improve, terminate them.

Key Employees

A capable management team makes a company a much more attractive acquisition candidate. Any company that plans to sell within two years should make sure that it has a strong individual in each key management position. Who are your key employees? Who is really good? Who needs to be replaced? Which people should stay on board after the sale? A buyer will usually ask which employees are critical to keep.

After the sale does management plan to stay or leave? Normally, management will stay for a short period and potentially longer if the company and the manager are happy with the arrangement. Management should plan to stay on through the transition period, which is generally six months.

Think about how people issues might affect an eventual sale. Employees can quit. This issue is a major concern when the transaction process begins. It may be a smart idea to offer the key people incentives both for performance and for remaining with the company for a period of time.

Do you have a contingency plan in case the owner or CEO becomes incapacitated? What if there is a family emergency? Is your management team capable of continuing to run the company smoothly if the CEO is no longer there? Organize the company so that the business does not rely on one key person. These are not pleasant subjects but the smart business owner will have a plan in place. A good plan helps to preserve the value that you have created.

Get the Employment Agreements Right

It is smart to review the terms of employment, benefit plans and potential payments to employees in the case of a change of control. Preparation includes securing employment agreements with key managers including noncompete covenants. New employees should sign noncompete agreements too. Most buyers will want senior and technical employees to have signed a good, modern employment agreement.

If your company has stock options, make sure that the vesting schedule is appropriate in the case of a sale. In many cases, shares automatically vest upon sale of the business.

Stay Put Incentives

It is an excellent idea to devise incentives for management and key employees—so they stay on board and motivated during the sale process. Over the years, I have seen a variety of incentive plans to keep employees on board. Some companies offered straightforward cash bonuses, others offered stock, and others offered a percentage of the sale price. If it is a percentage of the sale price, a good plan is to allocate an amount to a bonus pool that is distributed to key employees. The type of incentive program that will work best for your company depends on the employees and management's relationship with them.

GET YOUR ADMINISTRATIVE PRACTICES RIGHT

Administrative matters include corporate procedures, policies, contracts, agreements and other records. Company policies and procedures should be documented. Most companies have processes that are not written down that should be. Documenting systems and procedures is a good discipline for any business.

Make a list of all of the company's assets including supporting schedules. Review all supplier contracts. It is a good practice to extend contracts and agreements as long as possible. Make sure that the company is in compliance with all regulatory requirements. Have well-documented systems for hiring and firing. Make sure that your employment agreements are up to date and organized.

Review the terms of your building lease and make sure the lease is not about to expire. Also, do not sign a long-term lease. Depending on the buyer, this may create a liability so try to maintain flexibility. If the buyer plans to continue in the same space, a lease at a less-than-market rate is viewed positively. However, if the buyer does not plan to continue in the space then a long-term lease becomes a liability. The company needs to address this issue for each buyer since they will typically have different plans.

If the company has any unresolved lawsuits or other legal issues, they must be resolved before beginning the sale process. A lawsuit is a deal killer. In addition, make sure any disputes between shareholders or management are resolved ahead of time.

Corporate Records

Make sure that your contracts and records are well organized. Document your compliance with all regulatory requirements. Make sure the board minutes are up to date and complete. It is easier to keep board minutes current as you go versus doing them later. Don't overpay your law firm to build the corporate record history at the last minute.

This state of readiness often reflects the personality of the founder or CEO. Some are highly disciplined and organized. Others relish a little chaos and are good at scrambling when they need to. Your team should be able to produce documents relatively quickly when asked. Be prepared so that you do not have to scramble at the last minute.

Get Your Website Right

Make sure that the company's website is up to date and that it accurately describes your company's business. It is important that your website communicate the right message to potential buyers.

There are several audiences for a website—customers, prospects, employees, etc. If a company is thinking about selling, it may need to change the perspective and tone of its website so that it presents well for potential buyers as well as for the other audiences.

Buyers check out a company's website early on and first impressions are important. In my experience, most companies' websites are only average. The graphics may be interesting, but the message is often not clear. Many are outdated and do not accurately reflect the company's current focus. Sometimes the emphasis is inaccurate with respect to the company's current business model and customer set.

GET YOUR OPERATIONS RIGHT

Make sure that you have sound processes and procedures in place for the important aspects of your operations. These procedures should be written down so that new employees will understand your procedures. You do not want to have the correct procedures solely in the head of one of your employees. Printed manuals are a good idea. You want your processes systematized so that they are easily repeatable.

Use industry best practices whenever possible. This gives buyers confidence that the business is being run well. Make sure that your business practices do not raise any red flags.

Ensure that your information technology systems are up to date and well documented. Documentation of IT systems is an area that often receives poor marks from potential buyers.

Focus the company's efforts on the most profitable market sectors, the most profitable product lines and the most profitable customers. Get rid of all extraneous product lines and pet projects. Eliminate all expenses that are not business related. Make sure that you do not have any nonperforming assets. In addition, sell or dispose of any assets that will not be sold with the company.

Make sure that the company's office space and other building areas are clean, organized and uncluttered. When a potential buyer walks through your office he or she will develop an opinion about the business based on how it looks. You want that opinion to be a favorable one.

GET YOUR INTELLECTUAL PROPERTY RIGHT

Intellectual property (IP) is becoming an increasingly important aspect for the sale of many companies. One of the biggest problems that can derail the sale of a technology company is poorly documented intellectual property. If the ownership of the IP is in question, the transaction will not take place. I have been down this road before and it is not a pleasant situation.

The IP should be properly documented with particular attention to ownership issues. It must be crystal clear what software is owned and what software is licensed. In addition, make sure that the licenses are transferable. Make sure that you have access to all of the company's agreements. The buyer will want to review them during the due diligence phase. Prepare schedules of all patents, trademarks and copyrights. It is better to get these documents together earlier in the process rather than later.

Software documentation is another important matter. The company should have a documented quality control system for software design specifications, design reviews, risk analysis, code reviews and so on.

The due diligence process can be an extremely time-consuming and sometimes painful process. There will be fewer surprises and due diligence will proceed more smoothly if the company is prepared ahead of time.

Sometimes a company will decide to spin off some of its technology or a product line so it can focus on its most profitable products. Selling off a technology is possible but it is a more difficult task than selling a company because there are no revenues associated with it.

Given the increasing importance of intellectual property, it is a good policy to assign the task of managing the IP to a person on your team who is fairly responsible and organized, perhaps the CFO.

The last three chapters have dealt with administrative and financial issues; it is time now to move forward with actually improving the value of your company.

11 IMPROVE YOUR VALUE

If you plan to sell your business in the next two to four years, it is a good idea to start managing for maximum value right now. Put proactive plans in place to create the most value. In this chapter we discuss how to improve your value.

The primary way to boost value is to figure out ways to increase your profitability. Make sure that each one of your products contributes to your firm's profitability. Make sure that every customer contributes to your profitability as well. Increasing recurring revenues and maintenance revenues also builds value.

Other ways to enhance value are indirect but they are still important. Reducing the amount of working capital required increases value. Minimizing potential liabilities might increase value; but more importantly, it keeps value from going down. In addition to being a sound business practice, having accurate financial reporting systems makes the company more valuable.

The second principal way to increase value is to reduce the risks and that is the subject of the next chapter.

INCREASE RECURRING REVENUE

Increasing the amount of recurring revenue is an excellent way to boost value. Recurring revenue includes renewals, subscriptions, maintenance revenues, etc. A high level of recurring revenue means less risk for the buyer because it has a greater assurance that the revenues will be there next year. Recurring revenues have a greater degree of certainty. It is significantly easier for a company to renew a service with current customers than to make sales to new customers.

Many technology companies have revenue that is comprised of two parts—new sales and recurring revenues. Software as a service is a good example. Under this model, customers license software on a subscription basis and pay a monthly or annual fee. It typically renews every year. A buyer will be very interested in your renewal rates. Make sure that you compile this data accurately and have it readily available.

Think about innovative pricing models and other incentives to encourage customers to sign up for maintenance agreements. Increasing the amount of maintenance and support revenue is a good way to increase ongoing revenues.

PRODUCT PROFITABILITY

Take a good hard look at your product mix and make sure that all your products are profitable. This seems like a simple task but I have encountered many companies that have products or services that actually lose money. Their financial systems do not track profitability by product. The first step is to put tracking systems in place; then eliminate any products or services that lose money.

Sell off any obsolete or slow-moving inventory. It may be painful to sell inventory at low prices but it will free up cash and reduce carrying costs.

CUSTOMER MIX AND PROFITABILITY

First of all, make sure that your customer relationships are strong. A company that is thinking about selling must keep its customers at all costs and reduce the risk of customers leaving. There is nothing worse than losing customers during the sale process.

Move customers to multi-year contracts. Encourage them to sign up for longer contracts by offering special incentives and reducing prices. Increasing the length of customer contracts improves the certainty that your customers will continue to be customers in the future. During due diligence a buyer will examine your customer contracts so it is a good idea to extend these contracts. If customers have verbal agreements for certain services or preferences, put these agreements in writing.

How profitable is each customer? Many businesses cannot answer this question. You might have customers that actually cost you money and are not profitable. Institute a system to acquire this information; it is critical to ensure that you do not have customers that are costing you money.

Diversify your customer base. If a few customers account for a significant portion of your revenues, this will negatively impact value. Such a company is significantly riskier than one with a diversified base of customers.

Review your competitive situation. Make sure that you understand and can communicate exactly how you match up against competitors. A buyer will do its own competitive analysis and it should be consistent with your competitive assessment.

REDUCE WORKING CAPITAL

Working capital is an area that many companies do not have a good handle on. As you remember, working capital is defined as a company's current assets minus current liabilities. Every business has an optimum amount of working capital that is required to run the business. The appropriate amount depends on a company's industry, geography and a few other factors.

A buyer will examine the amount of working capital that a company has historically required. Working capital is typically analyzed as a percentage of revenues. A buyer will use the average for the last three or four years. If the buyer must invest additional working capital, that effectively increases the cost of the acquisition.

Give some thought to how you can decrease the amount of working capital required for your business. Inventory and accounts receivable are the two primary components of current assets. Do you have too much inventory on hand? If so, figure out a way to reduce inventory and you will reduce your working capital. Can you collect your accounts receivable more promptly?

Accounts payable are a big portion of current liabilities. Can you get better terms from your vendors? If you can stretch out your accounts payable it will reduce the amount of working capital required.

I was involved in one transaction in which the buyer and the seller had very different opinions about the correct amount of working capital. This became a major sticking point. The seller thought the amount of working capital should be small and the buyer thought it should be larger. (The seller was unrealistic about the correct amount.) They could not reach agreement and the transaction never did close.

If you are thinking about selling in the next few years, take steps to reduce the amount of working capital that is required. This will increase the value of your business.

MINIMIZE POTENTIAL LIABILITIES

Potential liabilities can be a serious problem in the sale of a company. In particular, off-balance-sheet liabilities can be problematic. Do everything in your power to identify and minimize potential liabilities. Even if they do not kill the transaction, they will reduce the price, sometimes significantly.

In one transaction, the selling company did not account for accrued vacation pay for its employees. The amount of accrued vacation pay had grown over the years but was not recorded on the balance sheet. (In this transaction the buyer was purchasing the seller's stock so it would be assuming all of the seller's liabilities.) The buyer was surprised and it lost some confidence in the seller and in the financial statements. The price had already been negotiated but now there was a glitch. The transaction eventually closed, but not without renegotiation and a slight reduction in the price.

As mentioned earlier, potential litigation is almost always a deal killer. If you have any potential litigation, do everything in your power to settle or eliminate this issue before you begin the process of selling the company.

Improving your value is critical for getting the best price, but just as important, is reducing your weaknesses and dealing with the risks that your company has. The next chapter addresses how to reduce risks and deal with weakness.

12 REDUCE YOUR RISKS AND WEAKNESSES

There are two primary ways to increase the value of a business—increase profits and reduce risk. Entrepreneurs certainly realize that increasing profits enhances the value of their businesses. But some don't consider the impact that risk plays in how a buyer assesses value.

Every company has some areas of risk and some areas of weakness. When selling a company, the key is to manage these areas effectively. How should you handle negatives? How should you manage questionable items? The sooner a company is realistic about its areas of weakness, the sooner it can address them.

Many CEOs and founders underestimate the degree of risk that surrounds their businesses. This is generally a good thing. If entrepreneurs focused on the risks instead of the opportunities, they would never have started their companies in the first place. However, when the time is right to sell, a realistic assessment of the risks will enable a seller to be prepared for a buyer's questions.

DEALING WITH PROBLEM AREAS

The first step is to recognize a problem area and admit that you have an issue. Do not gloss it over. You should anticipate the questions that a buyer will ask and provide the information that will put that objection to rest. It is important to be upfront about any weaknesses. Do not be defensive.

One of the things that we address in our exit strategy advisory service is pointing out issues that can raise red flags as well as identifying areas of weakness. You should deal with these issues early on because you don't want to be surprised when you first meet with a buyer. It pays to detect hidden problems and unforeseen problems in advance.

For each question about risk or weakness, the company must have a good explanation. The reasons cannot be fluffy or vague; they must be true and accurate. Don't state that your technology is the best if it is not truly the best. The buyer will eventually find out anything and everything about your company so upfront honesty will go a long way. You might as well be frank about it. There are no perfect companies. Being straightforward will help build a relationship with the buyer based on truthfulness and this is a good thing.

One of the best ways to deal with a weakness is to recognize that a weakness of the selling company may be an opportunity for the acquiring company. A good example is sales and marketing. Working with many technology and software companies over the years, I have found that sales and marketing is not their strong suit. In fact, they are often weak in this area. Weak sales and marketing is sometimes the very reason that the company is seeking to be acquired—they can't get enough market traction. The buyer is usually a larger company with better sales and marketing capabilities. The opportunity for the buyer is that it can increase sales of the products by selling them through the buyer's distribution channels.

TYPES OF RISK AND WEAKNESS

Companies face a wide range of risks. They confront market risk, technology risk, product risk, management risk, financial risk and other types of risk. How can you minimize these risks for the buyer? What can you do to address risk proactively?

Buyers will have a number of questions regarding your risks. Some might be areas of weakness rather than risk; however, the questions are appropriate for either one. For simplicity we refer to them as risk areas.

Customer Risks

Customer concentration is the biggest customer risk. If a significant portion of the company's revenues are derived from only a few customers, revenues could take a hit if a customer leaves.

Buyers worry about several things. Will the company lose any of its current customers? How difficult it will it be to get new customers? Are customers happy with the products and services that the company provides?

In one transaction that I was involved in, the major customer accounted for 30 percent of revenues. The buyer viewed this as a huge risk. What if the client left? In this case, I recommended that the seller stay close to this customer, inform them of the sale situation and do whatever it could to keep the customer happy. The strategy worked. Early in the due diligence process the buyer met with the customer and was reassured that the customer would stay with the business. The customer realized that the buyer was a larger firm with greater resources and it could do an even better job of meeting its needs.

Market Risks

In many transactions the buyer is a company in the same market or in an adjacent market so they understand the market risks. Risks loom much larger if a company is looking in from the outside. The key market questions include:

- Is the company's primary market growing, steady or declining?
- Will revenues continue to grow? What is the risk of revenue declining?
- Are margins deteriorating?
- What is the competitive situation?

Product risks are related to market risks. Does the company have a complete set of products? Are new products being developed? Are any products becoming obsolete?

Management Risks

Management risk includes areas such as management depth and stability. Does the company have a complete management team?

Are there areas where management needs to be hired or replaced? Will the current management team stay in place? If not, are there people to fill the important positions? What is the risk of key employees leaving? Make sure that the "keeper of relationships" is not leaving. This point can be best illustrated with an example. A friend was a successful company owner. She had a business partner; however, she was the primary salesperson and point person for the company. She was well known in the industry sector and everyone knew her at the trade shows. In other words, she was the face of the company.

She knew that she would eventually be selling the business and realized that when it came time to sell, any buyer would want her to stay on because she was so important. She also realized that after she sold the company she wanted to go do different things, not continue working at the company. She made the decision to step back from the limelight so that she and the company would not be synonymous. She hired a new sales manager and gradually stepped back from being the keeper of relationships. The transition worked out well and she successfully sold the company a few years later.

Operating Risks

Are the company's operating procedures sound? Does the company follow industry best practices? Do new processes and procedures need to be put in place? Don't rely on a few people who keep your business practices in their heads; build your business around repeatable procedures.

Just as a high customer concentration increases risk and reduces value, the same is true when a company is overly reliant on a single supplier. Even if it costs a little more, it's a good idea to have several suppliers for important parts and subassemblies.

Financial Risks

We discussed financial reporting systems earlier but let us review a few key questions that a buyer will be sure to ask. Are the company's cash flows adequate to meet its needs? Is it paying its bills on time? Will additional funds be required to maintain a desired level of working capital?

Is the capital equipment in good shape? Will machinery or equipment need to be replaced? Will additional capital expenditures be necessary? Does the company have any off-balance-sheet liabilities? In Chapter 9 we discussed the importance of having a reliable financial reporting system. Sound financial statements reduce risk in the buyer's eyes since there is more certainty about the company. This confidence carries over to other aspects of the business.

Now we shift our attention from looking internally at a firm's operations and risks to exploring how to view your markets strategically.

Thomas Metz

13 VIEW YOUR MARKETS STRATEGICALLY

A strategic buyer will pay a higher price than a financial buyer, so this section emphasizes how to think about your markets strategically. In order to view your markets strategically you must ask three questions:

1. Which market sectors are relevant?
2. Where is the movement in the market?
3. Who are the buyers in those sectors?

The process for seeking strategic buyers is more of an exploration than a precise search. More than one market sector may contain good buyers, so explore multiple adjacent markets and multiple sectors.

Market movement is one of the most important aspects of viewing your markets strategically. Movement in the markets can determine the best buyers. A buyer that has decided to enter a market sector will likely pay the highest price—to get into that sector quickly and forcefully.

THE MOVING MARKETS

Markets are always on the move. Markets expand; markets contract and markets go away. Sometimes markets move quickly and other times markets move slowly. Eventually, almost all market sectors will morph.

Notice the changes that are taking place. Pay attention to where the market is headed and which sectors are growing. Try to discern if any market niches are shrinking or if any new niches are being created. Recognizing movement is a critical aspect of viewing markets strategically.

Look for the movement of the entire range of players—buyers, competitors, future competitors and adjacent market companies. Observe the movement by potential buyers. Are they moving toward your market sector? Do your market sectors complement, or overlap, those of potential buyers? These questions are challenging; but make the effort to consider them.

Market movement can change the landscape of potential buyers, sometimes rapidly. For example, a healthcare data company was thinking about selling because a buyer had offered to acquire it for $5 million. The board and investors thought the company could be worth more so they declined the offer. Over the next three years the markets changed dramatically. New competitors popped up and some of the customers went away. The board decided to sell and after an extensive sale process, we closed a transaction for $2 million. The company neglected to notice the movement in its market.

Market movement is similar to three states of an object in physics—position, velocity and acceleration. It is easy to recognize the *position* of a company in the market. *Velocity* can be recognized as well. Velocity may be fast or the velocity may be slow, but is not hard to recognize velocity.

Acceleration is a different story. It is more difficult to recognize acceleration. An accelerating object may appear to be far away and then then next thing you know, it is quite close. That is the nature of acceleration—it happens quickly. Ask yourself which market sectors could be accelerating. Situations can change quickly and you do not want to mischaracterize the market.

A good example of how markets morph is the market for municipal government software. The customers are cities and towns who are increasingly using software to manage their activities. Software for managing building permits is a good example. Initially this market was made up of many small software companies and there were no dominant players. Over several years these firms were acquired, merged or closed down as larger companies moved into this market. Eventually, most of the small firms went away and the market became dominated by two big companies and three minor players. Paying attention to market movement is imperative when contemplating an exit.

The Nonobvious Buyers

Sometimes the best buyers are not in a company's core market space, but in the little spaces off to the side, in neighboring areas. Don't assume that you know who the best buyers are. Sometimes nonobvious buyers in adjacent markets can be excellent buyers. An adjacent market is a market space that touches on the primary market. Every market typically has about seven adjacent markets. Buyers in adjacent markets often use acquisitions as a way to enter new markets, gain new technology and new customers. An acquisition can give them a foothold in a new sector. A buyer can enter a market sooner, often less expensively and with less risk.

Creating a market map is a helpful tool to recognize the state of the market. A market map depicts your primary market and the sectors that border it. When selling a company, I generate a market map that illustrates the primary market with a handful of adjacent markets.

SIZE MAKES A DIFFERENCE

The size of potential buyers is an important consideration when viewing markets strategically. Some markets are comprised of many small companies, some markets are a mix of small and midsized companies and some markets are comprised of midsized and large companies. Markets that are polarized, with a handful of small companies at one end and a handful of large companies at the other end, produce a difficult situation for selling a company.

Many Small Companies

A market in this state consists of many small companies, perhaps as many as several hundred small firms across the United States. These markets are often young markets. As markets mature, consolidation occurs and many of these small firms are either acquired or go away and the larger companies take notice and move in.

The problem with markets comprised of many small companies is that there are few good buyers. A small company is not a good buyer because they don't have the cash or resources to make an acquisition. This is why midsized and large companies are the best buyers—they have the resources to do so.

All Big Companies

When the market consists of only a handful of large companies, this is a sign of a mature market and selling a company is more difficult. Large companies have their own technologies and large customer bases. An acquisition must be at least $25 million or $50 million in size to be of interest to them. Occasionally a large firm will acquire a small company to acquire vital technology, enter a new geographic area, or to get a foothold in a niche market but they are not interested in acquiring a small firm for its customer base.

A Few Midsized Buyers

Midsized buyers are the best buyers for acquisitions of companies less than $50 million. These midsized companies want to become big companies and growing via acquisition is an excellent strategy for them. These companies usually have adequate cash for acquisitions and some have a publicly traded stock that is good acquisition currency. Acquisitions are often part of their strategic plans.

The Perils of Polarized Markets

A market that is not polarized will consist of companies of many sizes. There will be a few large firms, a handful of midsized companies and a number of small companies. These markets are good for selling companies because there are buyers of various sizes, thus providing numerous alternatives.

A polarized market is one in which companies move toward the poles—small companies at one end and large companies at the other end. As markets mature they tend to become polarized. A polarized market will have three to five large companies at one extreme and a number of small companies at the other extreme and few or no midsized companies. The problem is that there are few good buyers (midsized companies) in a polarized market.

In one example, I was seeking a buyer for a firm that had developed software for managing the operations of distribution companies. This market was totally polarized with several hundred small companies dispersed across the country and four big national firms. The large firms had their own software solutions and did not care about adding a handful of additional customers. So the large companies were not viable buyers. The small firms could not afford to make an acquisition and there were no midsized companies in this market. As a result, there were no viable buyers and the software company decided to continue building its business.

The above section underscores the importance of viewing markets strategically. If the market shifts to become mature or polarized, the number of likely buyers decreases dramatically. The best time to sell is when there are a number of midsized buyers. A company seeking an exit should keep a watchful eye on the state of the market because it can have a dramatic impact on the price and outcome.

In the next chapter we explore the seventh step to achieving the maximum value—being prepared for, and responding intelligently to, an offer to acquire your company that comes in out of the blue.

Thomas Metz

14 BE PREPARED FOR AN UNSOLICITED OFFER

An offer to acquire your company may arrive unexpectedly. You should be ready if an offer comes in out of the blue and ready to respond intelligently.

Receiving an unsolicited offer is a fairly common occurrence for many companies. The offer may not be an official letter or for a specific price. Sometimes the CEO of the buyer may simply place a phone call to the CEO of the target company asking if they would be open to a sale. When a buyer knocks on your door it is smart to take them seriously.

Unsolicited offers come in several varieties. The first is an offer that is extremely good. The target has an instinctive sense that this is an excellent price and the best buyer. The second situation is one in which the offer appears to be pretty good and the target should seriously consider it; but, perhaps they should seek other offers as well. The third situation is one in which the seller thinks that the offer is lower than what another buyer might offer.

Everyone is flattered, of course, when a buyer is interested in your company. But how should a company respond? Should you scramble to get competitive offers? How should you contact other buyers? These are questions that a company should be prepared to answer.

Many times, companies are not sure how to respond. They think that trying to get additional offers is either difficult, risky, will take too long or will displease the buyer. The best action is to assess the situation and respond appropriately.

THE FIRST STEP—ASSESS

When you receive an unsolicited offer, a company should assess three areas:

- Assess your company
- Assess the market situation
- Assess the buyer

Assess Your Company

Assemble your management team and review your growth plan. Are you making good progress on your plan? Will you need additional capital for growth? Are your products or technology fully developed?

Review your marketing and sales efforts. Are you attacking the market effectively? Are you winning the competitive battles? Perhaps being part of a larger company be a good way to enhance your marketing and sales capabilities.

If your firm is growing nicely and building market share, it may be wise to sell later on. On the other hand, if your company is struggling to gain market traction or maintain profitability, selling now might be a good move.

Assess the Market

The second step is to assess the market situation. What is the stage of the market—is it early stage or a mature market? Is the market growing? Are new companies entering the market? Examine the adjacent markets. Do these sectors contain other buyers that could benefit from the acquisition of your company in order to enter your market?

Assess the Buyer

Do you think that the buyer making the offer is the best buyer? How good is the fit between your companies? Is the buyer already in your sector or about to enter it? Does the buyer have the ability to pay an attractive price? Are there other buyers that might be a better fit? Does the buyer have competitors that might be good potential buyers for your company?

THE SECOND STEP—RESPOND

It is a good idea to begin a dialog with the buyer that approached you and see where the conversation goes. However, going down this road can be a time-consuming process. It is best to bring in a professional at this point. An adviser can give you objective advice and provide a perspective on the market that will help you to decide the best course of action.

My recommendation is almost always to generate a few additional offers. How else will you know if you're getting the best price? The key question is how much time you can afford to take in generating additional offers.

There are three alternatives for responding to an unsolicited offer: the rapid response, the measured response, and the extended response.

Rapid Response—Contact 5 to 10 Companies

The rapid response involves immediately contacting a handful of likely candidates. The idea is to get several competitive bids as soon as possible so as not to impair the relationship with the first bidder. With a high-quality buyer in hand, you do not want to dally too long. This process should be conducted quickly.

The rapid response involves reaching out to five or 10 companies to ensure that you are getting the best price and terms. This process should take approximately three or four weeks.

Measured Response—Contact 10 to 20 Companies

In this situation, begin discussions with the first buyer and reach out to some additional buyers. Quickly draft a memorandum that describes the company. It does not need to be lengthy but it should accurately portray the firm and its strengths. This document is an excellent tool for putting the company's best foot forward.

Seek out 10 to 20 companies, going beyond the obvious candidates and make sure to contact companies in adjacent markets. The value of competitive bids is significant. The measured response typically lasts between four and six weeks.

Extended Response—Contact More Than 20 Companies

The extended response involves a fairly extensive search to identify additional buyers. In this situation, I might contact 20 to 40 companies. The time line for this approach is longer but it leaves no doubt that all of the best buyers have been contacted. The time frame for the extended response ranges from six to 10 weeks.

The next section discusses potential problem areas, why companies might not sell and the top 10 seller mistakes. Problems are a given for any sale-of-company transaction. Some obstacles are small and some are large, but there will always be hurdles to overcome.

Part III. Potential Problems

15 POTENTIAL PROBLEM AREAS

There is no end to the list of potential problems that can derail a transaction. Some problems can make it messy, some problems can cause delay and some can kill a transaction. Sometimes you can resolve an issue before it develops into a serious problem and other times you must deal with the problems as they arise.

Almost every deal blows up at least once. After verbal agreement, there is only about a 60 percent chance of successfully closing the transaction. The typical transaction will have not just one problem, but several problems. And they all have to be solved before the deal gets done.

Problems fall into several categories. The primary ones are financial problems and shareholder problems. Issues can arise regarding intellectual property, technology, products and customers. Problems can also pop up regarding contracts, environmental issues and litigation. Hidden liabilities can be an unwelcome surprise. Occasionally a transaction is going nicely from the seller's side and a problem occurs on the buyer's side.

This chapter reviews a number of the problem areas that can delay or torpedo a transaction.

FINANCIAL PROBLEMS

Financial problems are some of the worst problems. Revenues can fall off. Profits can take a downturn. Pricing levels may be difficult to maintain. Increased competition can put pressure on margins.

67

The realities of the markets can be cruel.

A decline in revenues, or even a slowdown in growth, raises questions for the buyer. They will wonder if the decline is temporary or is it an indicator of longer term problems. A buyer will question the probability of revenues and profits continuing for the next five years.

Hidden liabilities can be a deal killer. Also referred to as *off-balance-sheet-liabilities*, these problems are a concern in many transactions. A hidden liability can be anything from accrued vacation pay, to a sexual harassment suit in the wings or an environmental liability waiting to be exposed. The potential for hidden liabilities is one of the reasons that the due diligence process is so demanding.

Forecasts can cause problems too. If the forecast is not optimistic, it appears as if the company is not growing sufficiently. If the forecast is too aggressive, the seller may not be able to live up to its predictions during the sale process. Both are bad situations. Make sure that your forecasts are based on extremely reasonable assumptions with realistic revenue projections, realistic gross margins and realistic expenses. The company must be able to support its forecasts with assumptions that are absolutely reasonable.

CEO MISALIGNMENT

A situation we see from time to time is when the CEO's stock options are not yet in the money. In other words, the CEO will profit only if the company is sold at a high valuation. This situation can be subtle because it may not surface until late in the negotiations. A president may be financially better off by running the business and earning an attractive salary. His or her equity stake may be too small for him to act like a true shareholder. The lesson is to make sure the CEO's interests are truly aligned with those of the shareholders.

In some cases the CEO may not want the company to be sold. Ego can be a problem. Sometimes a president sees a sale as a kind of failure and he doesn't want to admit failure. He or she believes that with just a little more time and more capital, success will be right around the corner.

SHAREHOLDER ISSUES

Shareholder issues can be troublesome. Unfortunately, shareholder issues occur more often than one might think. A transaction has enough issues to contend with without involving the shareholders and their squabbles. The most common shareholder concern is, of course—who gets how much?

Many technology companies have venture capital firms as shareholders. Most venture capital firms have liquidity preferences regarding the return of their capital. Liquidity preferences can be two or three times the amount of the capital invested. In other words, if a venture capital firm invested $5 million in a company, a two times liquidity preference (upon sale of the company) means that the venture capital firm gets the first $10 million of sale proceeds. The remaining proceeds are split according to the ownership of common shares.

When a company sells for a high price, there are rarely any shareholder issues. Problems occur when the company sells for a low or medium price. I have seen situations in which the common shareholders received nothing. Either the venture capital firm had preferences or the company had liabilities that exceeded the sale price. When the common shareholders receive little, they have no incentive to vote in favor of a transaction. It may be wise for the preferred shareholders to allocate a portion of their proceeds to the common shareholders.

There are three primary lessons to be learned from the shareholder problems that I have experienced:

- Every shareholder problem must be resolved completely *before* a buyer makes an offer.
- Do not use complicated financial structures. Sometimes smart technology people get too clever and too complicated. A simpler structure is usually a better structure.
- Founders need to understand the implications of their decisions when raising capital. If the company does not achieve its growth objectives, the fine print of the financing agreement can be an unwelcome surprise.

INTELLECTUAL PROPERTY CONCERNS

Intellectual property is becoming increasingly important in the sale of companies. The licensing and ownership of all software and technology should be well documented. It should be evident what software is owned and what software is licensed. Have copies of all agreements and prepare schedules of patents, trademarks and copyrights. If the ownership of the intellectual property is in question, it can cause serious problems. If intellectual property is a key asset that is being acquired, it is imperative that the ownership be perfectly clear. We discussed this issue in Chapter 10; however, we make the point again here because intellectual property is such an important issue.

TECHNOLOGY PROBLEMS

Technology issues can crop up in several ways. Technology can become obsolete in a short time period. It may be built on an old platform and not embody the latest technological developments. If a company cannot afford to keep its technology current, the firm should consider selling earlier in its life. Waiting until its technology is no longer up to date can be a fatal mistake.

Occasionally, compatibility with industry standards can be an obstacle. Sometimes a company will develop its own unique technology. When the time comes to sell, this unique technology may be a disadvantage if it does not conform to the buyer's technology.

Licensing issues can cause problems. The seller may have licensed software that is included in its products. The company must make sure that these licenses are transferable to a buyer. Think ahead when licensing any technology, keeping in mind that this might be an issue when it comes time to sell the company.

PRODUCT PROBLEMS

Never exaggerate product capabilities. Occasionally sellers exaggerate product capabilities or the stage of product development. These matters are almost always discovered in due diligence. The seller should be sure to accurately communicate the stage of product development as well as product capabilities.

Inventory can be a problem as well. Inventory may be missing or obsolete. Keep accurate and up-to-date records of your inventory. Inventory that is even a few months old can become less valuable in a hurry.

In the sale of one manufacturing company there was a problem with obsolete inventory. The buyer had acquired the assets including the inventory. After the transaction closed, the buyer discovered that some of the inventory included older products that retailers no longer carried. The seller had represented that the entire inventory was in good condition and none was obsolete. The buyer threatened to sue and the seller paid the buyer for the amount of obsolete inventory.

CUSTOMER ISSUES

Fear of losing customers is a common concern for a company that is seeking to sell. This is particularly worrisome when only a handful of customers make up the majority of the company's revenues. A customer that accounts for 15 percent or more of the company's revenues is a concern.

It is critical to stay close to your customers. My advice is to be up front with your most important customers and inform them fairly early of your decision to sell. The buyer will definitely want to speak with key customers. The earlier the customer is advised of the situation the better they will feel about being important and trusted.

Sometimes an agreement for the company's services will have a clause stating that if there is a change in control then the agreement is no longer in force. Check to see if your agreements are transferable between customers and the acquiring company.

CONTRACT CONCERNS

A selling company should review each contract to determine if any issues need to be dealt with. Typical contracts include customer contracts, building leases and equipment leases. Make sure that your important contracts can be assumed by the buyer.

If the seller has a long-term building lease, it may be a

problem if the buyer does not want to remain in that space. Lease rates typically increase over time so the seller can often sublease the space. However, if rates have fallen, the seller will take a hit when subletting and will have to make up the difference to the buyer.

The seller may have leased some of its equipment—computers, postage machines, copiers, telephone systems and other equipment. The buyer may or may not need this equipment and any existing equipment leases must be dealt with.

LITIGATION ISSUES

Litigation or pending litigation is the ultimate deal killer. Even the potential for litigation can ruin a transaction. *Indirect* litigation can have a negative effect as well. For example, one company that I was involved with had licensed certain technology from another firm. The other firm was being sued by a third company regarding its technology. The seller decided to put the sale on hold until this legal issue was resolved. Very few buyers will move forward with a transaction if there are any litigation issues hanging over the target. These matters must be settled at almost any cost.

ENVIRONMENTAL SNAGS

Environmental issues can put a serious damper on a transaction. Most companies don't have environmental issues, but if they do, the consequences can be deadly. The problem is that environmental issues do not go away easily and they can be expensive to rectify. The cost of cleaning up an environmental problem (i.e., remediation) is difficult to estimate. By law, the liability transfers to the buyer. Rarely will a buyer move forward with an acquisition until the environmental issues have been completely resolved.

PROBLEMS ON THE BUYER'S SIDE

The seller is not the only party who can have problems that delay or halt a transaction. The buyer may have trouble raising cash or they may experience shareholder and management problems.

For example, this transaction was proceeding on schedule; the due diligence was complete and the transaction was looking good. The closing documents were almost finished and signing was only a week away. The buyer for this software firm was McAfee Associates, the antivirus software company. A new CEO had come on board at McAfee a week before the closing date. The first thing he did was nix this deal; he had different ideas about McAfee's direction. After six months of work and an extensive market search it was dead in the water.

So it was back to the drawing board. The story had a happy ending—a few months later we sold the company to a Texas software firm that needed new software products to spur its growth. We closed the deal and the founder was able to retire after a long and successful career in the software business.

The list of difficulties that can delay or kill a transaction is extensive. This chapter has reviewed the most common problems. Every transaction will encounter a variety of hurdles and problems. The best a seller can do is to be aware of potential difficulties and prepare diligently before beginning the process.

Next we review the top 10 seller mistakes. The list could be much longer, but these are the most common and the lessons are instructive.

Thomas Metz

16 TOP 10 SELLER MISTAKES

Company owners and CEOs make a number of mistakes when selling their companies. This chapter reveals the ten most common mistakes that I have observed over many years of selling companies.

THE TOP 10 LIST

1. Confusing Price with Value
2. Unrealistic Price Expectations
3. Trying to Sell at the Top
4. Waiting Too Long to Sell
5. No Real Exit Strategy
6. Not Engaging a Professional
7. No Competitive Bids
8. Poor Negotiation Problem Solving
9. Not Prepared for Unsolicited Offer
10. Neglecting Day-to-Day Operations

1. CONFUSING PRICE WITH VALUE

To close any transaction, the parties simply need to agree on price. They do not need to agree on value. Price is necessary; value is not. Different buyers will have various ideas about the value of a company. Value is in the eye of the beholder. In fact, values can vary dramatically depending on the strategic importance to a particular buyer.

Do not get locked into valuation formulas. For the most part they are irrelevant when selling a company with strategic value. In the technology markets, value is strategic; it is not based on financial results. By the way, multiples of revenue are irrelevant. A buyer may speak in terms of revenue multiples but they do not think in terms of revenue multiples. A company is worth whatever a buyer is willing to pay.

2. UNREALISTIC PRICE EXPECTATIONS

Unrealistic price expectations can derail a good transaction. A savvy buyer will recognize early on that a seller is asking too much and they will walk away. Savvy buyers have learned that an unrealistic seller can be a huge waste of time.

Unseasoned negotiators make the mistake of thinking that if they ask a high price, they will be more likely to obtain a high price. This is rarely the case. In a strategic transaction there is no "true" value of the business. The business is worth what a buyer will pay for it. Get as many offers as you can and then take the highest one.

3. TRYING TO SELL AT THE TOP

Do not try to sell at the top or even just before the top. Why not? Because you will never know where the top is. This is an impossible question to answer.

The ideal time to sell is when the larger companies have the greatest need to acquire your company; when they want your business, assets or technology. Trying to pick the top usually results in missing the window and not selling for the optimal price.

Too many CEOs think about value in financial terms, not strategic terms. The mindset is: "If we wait, we will be worth more." For technology firms, the strategic value is typically greater than the financial value so waiting does not increase the value.

Markets are continuously changing; they are not static. The risks rarely diminish over time. The price that a company might command at one point in time may be very different from the price it commands a year later, even if the company is unchanged.

4. WAITING TOO LONG TO SELL

In my experience many companies wait too long before selling. There is always some excuse that keeps them from moving forward with a sale. They just want to get revenues up a little more, get the latest version of the product developed, attend the next industry trade show, or whatever. Venture capital firms are guilty of waiting too long as well. Venture capitalists are in the business to hit home runs, not singles or doubles. So they typically wait too long, hoping for that home run.

Waiting for better financial performance is not usually a good plan. For a company with strategic value, the buyer is seeking technology and capabilities, not revenues or cash flow. Although better financial performance certainly helps, the transaction does not hinge upon financial results. The strategic asset is unchanged, even if revenues are slightly higher.

If you wait for revenues to peak, there may be little growth left. Do not try to wring every last dollar out of the market; sell when there is still growth for a buyer to realize. Buyers tend to be smart about the markets. Sooner or later they will realize that the company has milked the market dry. If they do make an offer, it will be a low offer. One of the cardinal rules of M&A is that a company should always sell before it needs to sell.

Entrepreneurs and CEOs are optimists and they believe they can grow their companies to the stars. If the company is performing well, the CEO wants to grow revenues even higher. If the company is doing OK, the CEO still wants to boost profits. If the company is struggling, the CEO wants to dig out of the hole and achieve profitability. There is no shortage of optimism; and there is always a reason to wait. This mindset can be a problem. It takes courage to sell.

The smart sellers are ruthlessly realistic about the market. They recognize early on when larger competitors are entering their markets, putting pressure on prices and margins. The right time to sell is when the market is ready.

77

5. NO REAL EXIT STRATEGY

An effective exit strategy increases the probability of a successful exit. It means that the company is operating smoothly and has few areas of weakness. For a prepared company, the sale process will be less stressful and less disruptive.

A good exit strategy can impact management decisions in the short term. For example, perhaps product development decisions should be reconsidered in light of an exit. Thinking about the exit gives the board of directors a reason to review the alignment between shareholder groups and management. Should the growth strategy to be focused on longer-term or shorter-term objectives?

Keep a strategic eye on the market. As we discussed earlier, the top price is achieved when potential buyers desire your company the most. This is a function of market timing which may be different than your internal timing.

Many companies do not plan far enough in advance. They are too busy running day-to-day operations to take time to reflect on their eventual exit. A company should begin thinking about its exit plan and get its house in order if it plans to sell within four years.

6. NOT ENGAGING A PROFESSIONAL

A CEO who tries to sell his or her own company puts himself at a distinct disadvantage. There is no way a CEO can run the company and competently manage the sale process at the same time. The transaction will be shortchanged and mistakes can be costly. The CEO cannot aggressively push the transaction without appearing desperate. Plus, he or she can't possibly view the company objectively.

An objective third party can help defuse unreasonable claims, establish a constructive atmosphere and minimize extreme posturing. Friction can develop in negotiations. To avoid an adversarial relationship, let an intermediary handle the negotiations and be the bad guy.

Buyers do not want to waste their time with a seller who is not serious. A buyer will view a sale managed by the CEO as not being a serious seller. If the company was serious, it would engage an investment banking firm to professionally manage the process. The

CEO's job is to mind the store and keep the business running smoothly during the sale process. This is the best role for management and it creates the most value.

Transaction experience is the best reason for hiring a professional. The CEO or board members may have been involved in the sale of several companies, but an experienced investment banker will have been involved in many more transactions. In my case, I have been involved in the sale of more than 100 companies. This experience gives me the tools, skills and judgment to be extremely effective in closing transactions. Chapter 28 discusses this topic in more depth. There is no substitute for extensive transaction experience when selling a company.

7. NO COMPETIVE BIDS

Talking with only a few buyers is a mistake that many sellers make. The highest price is achieved when there are multiple buyers and competitive bids. Many selling companies make the mistake of not reaching out to enough potential buyers and not generating competitive offers.

Many firms presume that they know who the best buyers are because they know their market space. This mindset can be limiting; insiders can be blind to the edges of the market. These peripheries are where the emerging buyers exist. The only way to identify the complete set of buyers is to execute a disciplined market exploration.

Casting a wide net ensures that all potential buyers will be contacted. For example, my strategy is to execute a disciplined process and reach out to 75 to 150 potential buyers. I make sure to contact nonobvious buyers, often in tangential market sectors. As a result, I am confident that *all* potential buyers have been contacted. The more buyers, the greater the chance of receiving competitive offers.

8. POOR NEGOTIATION PROBLEM SOLVING

Overcoming problems and obstacles is an essential deal skill. About 40% of transactions fall apart at least once. Poorly solved problems can delay a deal or result in a suboptimal transaction structure.

It is important to understand how the other party views the problem. The stated problem may not be the real problem. Strive to understand the real reasons behind your opponent's positions.

Many problems have multiple solutions. Step outside the box; don't be too linear. Be aware of clinging to your assumptions. In fact, relaxing the assumptions is an excellent way to redefine the problem which opens the door to better solutions. Many tough problems can be solved with out-of-the-box and imaginative thinking.

9. NOT PREPARED FOR UNSOLICITED OFFER

More and more companies are being acquired early in their life cycles. Receiving an unsolicited offer is a common occurrence for technology companies. The buyer that first approaches you, however, may not be the best candidate.

How should a company respond to an offer out of the blue? Should you scramble to get competitive offers? The company must review its strategic plan, examine the market and assess the buyer. And then you must decide whether to contact a few additional buyers or numerous buyers. The topic of preparing for an unsolicited offer is addressed in depth in Chapter 14.

10. NEGLECTING DAY-TO-DAY OPERATIONS

Management should stay focused and run the business to the best of their ability. Missing the numbers or losing a big customer can cause real problems when trying to close a transaction. Buyers will lose confidence and that is not good.

The time period for selling a company may continue for six to 12 months. It is critical to keep revenues coming in, keep the sales pipeline full, keep expenses in check and employees and customers happy. Maintaining and growing customer relationships will add real value. Declining revenues will result in a lower purchase price. Management must remain keenly focused on running the business competently.

17 WHY COMPANIES DO NOT SELL

When a company fails to sell it is likely to be for one of four reasons:

- Price—the parties are too far apart on price. The seller's price expectations are not be in line with what the market is willing to offer.
- Problems—the transaction problems cannot be resolved to the satisfaction of both parties.
- Technology solved—the product advantage or technology issue has been solved in another way so that buyers do not need the selling company's solution.
- Polarized markets—a polarized market has few good midsized buyers.

Unrealistic expectations can dramatically impact the success of a company sale. When the asking price is too high, buyers balk at spending the significant time and effort required to evaluate an acquisition. Unrealistic expectations result from inappropriate comparables and shareholder issues. Management may have heard about the acquisition of a competitor at an exceptional price. The transaction may not be truly comparable to their company, but it sets a price expectation that can be hard to overcome.

When shareholder interests are not aligned, price expectations can get out of hand. For example, the shareholders may have lost patience and want liquidity but the CEO wants to continue building the company, he or she may be at cross purposes with the shareholders and therefore set too high a price. Sometimes the president's opinion of value is based on what the company *could be worth* rather than what it actually *is worth today*.

Earlier we discussed the myriad obstacles that can crop up during the sale process. If a problem cannot be solved, it must be minimized to the point where it does not impede the transaction from going forward. If too many problems are unresolved the transaction is unlikely to be completed.

The technology problem may have been solved. A company may have excellent products or technology, but if potential buyers have figured out another way to solve that issue, they do not need to make the acquisition. Buyers may have developed their own solution, licensed similar technology or acquired a competitor.

Timing is important. The first company in a market space to be acquired has an advantage because it has a solution that potential buyers need. If a company tries to sell too late, potential buyers may have already developed solutions. The lesson for management is to keep a sharp eye on competitive solutions in your market.

If a market is polarized, finding a suitable acquirer may prove difficult. There are few good midsized buyers in a polarized market. The large companies are rarely interested in small acquisitions and the small companies do not have the resources to make acquisitions.

Even after executing an extensive and disciplined sale process, some companies may not sell. It is essential to recognize the realities of the market.

Part IV presents an overview of the process for selling a company. This section gives the company owner a basic understanding of the principal issues and timeline. Topics include confidentiality, negotiations, transaction structures, the purchase agreement and due diligence. In addition we offer advice about engaging the appropriate attorney, accountant and investment banker.

Part IV. The Sale Process

18 OVERVIEW OF THE SALE PROCESS

Selling a company takes between six and twelve months to complete. Transactions can be closed in a shorter time if necessary, but a hurried transaction does not produce the best price. In some cases, a transaction may prolong for 18 months if there are major problems or issues with the buyers.

The investment banker's first task is to draft the descriptive memorandum. This document describes the company in some detail and includes input from the management team. Then the banker starts building the database of potential buyers, which could range from 75 to 150 companies depending on the market.

Contacting and interacting with potential buyers is the next step, a process that continues for three to five months. Interested buyers will request additional information about the company. They will participate in conference calls and visit the company. When a buyer is ready to make an offer, they will present a letter of intent that summarizes the basic terms of the transaction. If the seller accepts the terms, the buyer begins the due diligence process. Due diligence is an in-depth review of the company's business, financial statements, contracts and legal documents.

While due diligence is being performed, the attorney for the buyer drafts the purchase agreement—the legal documents that spell out the detailed terms of the transaction. When due diligence is completed and the buyer is satisfied, the closing documents are signed, the money is transferred and the transaction is complete.

UNDERSTANDING THE PROCESS

It is important that the seller clearly understand the process. Sellers usually ask the investment banker a number of questions about the sale-of-company process:

- How much time is required of the management team?
- What is the transaction time line?
- How should we handle confidentiality?
- What and when should we tell our employees?
- Do you plan to contact our competitors?
- How do you set a price for the company?

Certainly, there will be other questions as well. Management should discuss all their questions with the investment banker so that they have a thorough understanding of the process going forward.

The timeline for the process is illustrated below.

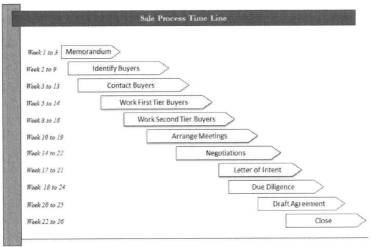

Figure 19.1 Sale Process Time Line

EXECUTING A DISCIPLINED PROCESS

One of the investment banker's roles is to assess the company with respect to the market. He pinpoints the company's strengths that acquirers are likely to be interested in. As the investment banker moves forward, he or she can provide valuable feedback to management about how the market views the company.

The Descriptive Memorandum

The first step in the sale of a company is to draft a descriptive memorandum. This document includes the basic information about the company: products and services, technology, markets, customers and distribution channels. It summarizes the backgrounds of the management team and includes summary financial information. It is important that the descriptive memorandum be complete and accurate. The memorandum may or may not contain confidential information.

There are two general approaches to confidentiality. The first is *not to include* any confidential information in the memorandum. Confidential information is provided later after a nondisclosure agreement (NDA) has been signed. This approach gives a buyer basic information about the company without the hassles of an NDA.

The second approach is to *include* confidential information in the memorandum. A buyer must sign an NDA prior to receiving any information. This approach keeps more information confidential; however, it slows down the process and is more cumbersome. The next chapter discusses confidentiality in more detail.

Identify and Contact Buyers

After the memorandum has been completed, the focus shifts to identifying and researching companies that might be good buyers. The investment banker begins building a list of potential acquirers. Management will suggest companies that it thinks might be good buyers as well.

The approach that I have found most effective is to cast a wide net and then work diligently to cull the list to a small set of well-qualified buyers. This disciplined and rigorous process works well in any market space. With this approach, I am confident that I have contacted all the good buyers. Sometimes bankers and management tend to overthink the market with preconceived ideas about who the best buyers are.

This process of contacting and interacting with buyers continues for several months. Some buyers need to be prodded along in the process since they are busy with their day-to-day business. The role of the investment banker is to drive the process and move buyers towards making an offer. This includes arranging conference calls and meetings with management. The objective is to end up with several companies that are interested in making offers to acquire the company.

The next step is negotiating the price and terms with each interested buyer. When value is highly strategic, the acquisition may be significantly more attractive to one buyer. Typically, the buyer and seller will verbally agree on the general structure of the transaction. Then the buyer will send a letter of intent that outlines the terms of the transaction.

The Pre-Closing Period
The period prior to closing is a crucial time for the selling company. This is when transactions tend to fall apart. Negative developments can reduce the price or even kill the transaction.

The seller should do everything in its power to keep revenues coming in and the sales pipeline full. It is imperative to keep customers satisfied, the employees happy, the management team fully engaged and avoid any setbacks.

Negotiating and Closing
After the letter of intent has been signed, there are three primary activities to complete: the due diligence review, the resolution of any outstanding issues and the drafting of the legal documents by the buyer's attorney. The closing process generally takes four to eight weeks and sometimes longer if due diligence questions need to be addressed.

There are a lot of moving parts in a sale-of-company transaction. Every transaction will involve a few surprises that pop up during the due diligence process. Even with very simple transactions, issues always arise. The fewer surprises there are, the better the odds of successfully closing the transaction.

At closing, the parties meet at the attorney's conference room and sign the documents. Dates are inserted into documents that had been left blank. Closing is usually accomplished in a couple of hours.

TWO TYPES OF SALE PROCESSES

There are two primary methods for managing the sale process: the negotiated sale and the two-step auction method. Each method has advantages and disadvantages.

The Negotiated Sale

The negotiated sale is the most effective process for selling companies with strategic value. It is also the best process for transactions in which the purchase price is less than about $30 million. In a negotiated sale, the investment banker contacts and negotiates with each company as if it were the only buyer.

The negotiated sale involves several steps. The investment banker contacts a wide range of potential buyers. He provides buyers with information about the company, arranges conference calls and meetings and moves the buyers forward. The banker attempts to get several buyers to make offers to acquire the company.

The negotiated sale is a more flexible process than the auction process. It does not involve hard and fast deadlines. This is one of the reasons that buyers tend to respond better to this process. The banker conducts negotiations with one or more buyers and the seller typically accepts the offer with the highest price and the most favorable terms.

The negotiated sale is more work than the two-step auction; however, it is the best way to complete strategic transactions.

The Two-Step Auction

The two-step auction method is better for larger transactions, greater than $30 million. The investment banker contacts a range of buyers and provides a basic information packet. He requests that buyers make an indication of interest and a preliminary offer by a specific date. After these preliminary offers are received, the banker selects the handful of buyers who made the highest offers to enter a second round of bidding.

The second round buyers will visit the company, meet with

management, review due diligence information and proceed to making final bids. The final bids are due on a specific date. The bidder with the best price and terms is selected and the parties move forward to sign the purchase documents.

The two-step auction process works well for companies with operating profits greater than $3 million. In these situations, the likely buyers are generally large companies with dedicated acquisition teams that can afford to spend the time and effort to evaluate potential acquisitions.

Some buyers do not like the auction process and they may not participate. The auction requires buyers to respond to specific time deadlines and there is a danger of overpaying. The benefit of the auction process is that it can get a transaction completed in a relatively short time frame.

One caveat: do not assume that the process that works for large transactions is also best for small transactions. For companies with strategic value, it is difficult for any buyer to make a meaningful preliminary offer. The target must be examined in depth for a buyer to fully understand its strategic value, which is a prerequisite to making a realistic offer.

19 CONFIDENTIALITY

Confidentiality is an important issue that must be addressed in the sale of any company. The appropriate level of confidentiality must be determined and put in place. The company also needs to decide how it plans to communicate with its customers and its employees. The level of confidentiality will vary depending on the situation.

Confidential information includes financial statements, trade secrets, software, engineering plans, customer lists, etc. Confidential information does not include information already in the public domain or information already known by the buyer. Sometimes even the fact that the company is for sale is confidential. There are tradeoffs between keeping the sale as confidential as possible and managing the process efficiently.

NONDISCLOSURE AGREEMENTS

Nondisclosure agreements (NDAs) are the primary means for protecting confidentiality. Although NDAs are standard agreements, there are usually a few clauses that one buyer or another will want to change. A large buyer will insist upon using their own NDA, not the one provided by the seller.

Most NDAs state that the buyer will not disclose confidential information to others. It usually does not prevent them from using this information internally. The best way to keep truly confidential information from a potential buyer is to not disclose it to them until it is absolutely necessary or not at all.

Using an NDA too early in the process can create obstacles. Management and attorneys can get bogged down in the details of the NDA, resulting in several weeks going by until agreement is reached.

COMMUNICATING WITH CUSTOMERS

CEOs are often concerned that customers and prospective customers will get wind of the potential sale and therefore not purchase the company's products. Competitors may spread rumors. This is one of the hazards of the sale process. Informing customers is a judgment call on management's part. It is probably best to inform your major customers.

Competitors are the potential buyers most likely to spread rumors. Because of this, the banker should postpone contacting competitors until later in the sale process.

COMMUNICATING WITH EMPLOYEES

Communicating with employees is an important decision as well. Employees are vital assets for most companies and it is imperative that they stay on board during the transaction process. It is a good idea to put retention bonuses in place to give management and key employees an incentive to stay on board.

Some CEOs will tell their full management teams early on in the process. Others will wait until later, and then, may confide in only a few individuals. For the non-key employees, it is less important and sometimes disruptive to mention a potential sale. There are pros and cons for each approach and each case is different.

The best advice I can give a CEO is to make this decision based on the level of trust and the relationship that he or she has with the employees. Sooner or later people will get wind of the situation. It is difficult to keep a secret like this for long. In my opinion, the best policy is for management to be open and honest with employees fairly early in the process.

For many sale transactions, the employees and customers will be better off. The company will likely be on stronger footing with greater financial resources.

20 NEGOTIATING THE DEAL

Negotiations are a combination of a chess game, a poker game and a dance. They are similar to chess because it is a sequence of moves and you are trying to outthink your opponent. Negotiations are like poker because you are interacting and bluffing and money is involved. They are like a dance because you move together and in the end the companies will be partners.

Negotiations are fluid situations. When negotiating the sale of a company with strategic value, there are no right or wrong answers. There are no true comparisons of multiples. Negotiating a strategic transaction requires an accurate understanding of the other party and of the market situation. A flexible negotiating style is more effective than having a preset strategy. Negotiating skill is critical because the price you get is the price you negotiate.

READ YOUR OPPONENT

Understanding your opponent and reading the other side are the cornerstones of good negotiations. In every negotiation that I am involved in, one of my primary objectives is to gain an accurate understanding of the buyer and his or her strategic objectives.

Probe to understand why the buyer is interested in making an acquisition. I go to great lengths to understand how the buyer views the seller's strategic assets. I want to know how valuable these assets are to them. I also try to figure out the buyer's framework for evaluation.

Look at the issues from both perspectives—yours and the

other party's. It is easier to convince someone using their framework and assumptions rather than yours.

NEGOTIATING SKILLS AND TACTICS

Be sure to get the order of the negotiation activities right. Make progress negotiating the broader issues first. Save the details for later. Too many people get sidetracked by negotiating details early on in the process.

Emphasize the areas of mutual interests. To get a dialogue going, introduce a few trial proposals. Anticipate concessions and plan a few in advance. Think several moves ahead and anticipate the reaction from the other side.

Be realistic about presenting a price range. Certainly you do not want to state a price that is too low, but the opposite is also true. Stating a price that is too high can signal the buyer that you are unrealistic and they might be wasting their time. It is better to set a price range that is relatively wide, rather than a specific amount. Sometimes a ballpark range will give the buyer some assurance that the seller is realistic.

The best negotiators are expert listeners. They pick up on nuances and these nuances are important because they give insight on how the other party views the situation. Be aware of emotion, both in your arguments and the other party's arguments. An emotional argument will beat a good logical argument most of the time.

Try to take your ego out of the equation. Do not let issues become personal. Use humor now and then to diffuse touchy situations. Patience is also a key negotiating skill. Sometimes it just takes some time for issues to be resolved. Occasionally, a negotiator needs to get tough and play hardball and the experienced negotiator recognizes when this is appropriate.

Be unconventional. A creative negotiator will seek unconventional approaches when solving problems. The key to this ability is to think outside the box. Viewing the problem in original ways is the key to developing creative solutions.

Inexperienced negotiators make several common mistakes. First they tend to focus only on their side of the situation; they do not fully understand the other party's point of view. They are not the best listeners and they cling to their assumptions a little too strongly. Another mistake is letting a large problem engulf the discussions. Use ingenuity and break a big problem into smaller issues that can be solved more easily.

Generating alternatives is an important part of strengthening your negotiating position. Alternatives might include contacting other buyers, raising capital, entering into a partnership or continuing on your current growth path. Alternatives are particularly important when you are negotiating with only one buyer.

My strong advice is that you should not enter into negotiations without having a professional advisor in your corner. There is no substitute for experience when selling companies. Most CEOs enjoy negotiating and the sale the company is no different. The problem is that often they don't know what they don't know; and they don't realize what they are not perceiving. They may not recognize that a key question was not asked or that a point was not brought up.

The buyer may have been down the acquisition path several times before with knowledgeable advisors and significant experience under their belt. You do not want to be outmatched. Bring in an experienced investment banker or advisor; he or she will pay for himself or herself many times over.

If you are interested in more about negotiating strategy, tactics and good practices, *Selling the Intangible Company*, devotes a chapter to this topic.

Thomas Metz

21 THE LETTER OF INTENT

The letter of intent is an excellent way for the buyer to communicate the basic transaction terms. Clearly communicating the terms is important for moving a transaction forward smoothly. Let us review the key terms in a letter of intent, often referred to as an LOI.

Sometimes the buyer drafts the letter as the first communication of its offer to the seller. In other cases, the letter is drafted after both parties have verbally agreed on the basic terms. The letter is usually drafted by the buyer.

A positive aspect of the letter of intent is that it demonstrates commitment by the buyer. A buyer will rarely send a letter of intent unless it has a serious intent to purchase the company.

The letter of intent describes the general price and terms that the buyer is offering. A well-drafted LOI is short, typically not more than about three pages. The letter should address the major points and not go into details. It should be simple and straightforward with minimal back and forth between the parties.

Most of the clauses in the letter are not binding; however, a couple of paragraphs typically are binding and the letter should state precisely what is binding and what is not.

In addition to the basic price and terms, the LOI includes information about not hiring away employees and a no-shop clause. In the no-hire clause the buyer promises not to try to hire any of the seller's employees. The no-shop clause is a promise by the seller not to contact other buyers during the period that the letter of intent is in effect, typically 45 to 90 days. The no-shop clause protects the buyer by giving them a window of time to perform their necessary due diligence. The promises made on these topics are usually binding.

For most transactions, a confidentiality agreement will already have been signed before the parties reach the LOI stage. If they have not signed one, the LOI should include binding confidentiality language.

The price is usually specified in dollar terms. The transaction structure should be specified as a "purchase of assets" or a "purchase of the outstanding shares" of the company. If the buyer is using its stock as the transaction currency, the LOI should state whether the price is a specific number of shares or whether it is a dollar amount of shares.

A target closing date should be specified, although this date can be changed later. The letter may include conditions to closing such as successful due diligence, legal issues and the signing of a definitive agreement. The LOI should also have an expiration date, usually two or five days in the future.

An important point to consider is that if a company does not want to be committed to one specific buyer, the seller should *not* sign a letter of intent.

22 TRANSACTION STRUCTURES

There are two fundamental types of transactions—stock sales and asset sales. A selling company can sell its stock or it can sell its assets. The buyer can pay with cash or pay with shares of its own stock. A transaction structure referred to as a stock deal is one in which the buyer purchases the stock of the selling company. An asset sale is a transaction in which the buyer purchases the assets of the seller; it does not acquire the corporate entity.

Transactions larger than $25 million are usually structured as a sale of stock. Smaller transactions are often structured as a sale of assets. This is not a hard and fast rule; however, I have seen a number of small transactions that were sales of stock.

SALE OF ASSETS

Selling assets is the simplest transaction structure. Assets include most of the assets of a company: desks, telephones, software, patents, trademarks, inventory, equipment, computers, accounts receivable, etc. The buyer will often assume some liabilities such as accounts payable.

Buyers prefer to purchase assets on small transactions because it reduces the possibility of unknown liabilities. The seller usually wants to sell stock and the buyer usually wants to purchase assets. What is favorable for the buyer is not favorable for the seller and vice versa.

If the selling company is a C Corporation, there are some negative aspects regarding selling its assets because the seller must pay taxes twice. The C Corporation itself must pay taxes on the gain for a sale of assets and then the shareholders must pay taxes when they receive the proceeds from the sale. S Corporations and Limited Liability Companies do not pay tax at the corporate level, so they are taxed only once.

This can be a significant matter. In one transaction that I was involved in, the deal actually fell apart because the buyer wanted to purchase assets, not stock. The selling company was a C Corporation and it had to pay taxes on the gain and then the three founders had to pay additional taxes individually. The proceeds that the founders would receive after taxes were not enough for them to want to go through with the transaction.

Assuming Liabilities

If purchasing assets, the buyer will assume selected liabilities of the seller. Assuming liabilities is a way for a buyer to raise the price of the transaction without having to put up additional cash.

It makes sense for the buyer to assume the accounts payable—because it wants to make sure the bills are paid. The buyer wants to maintain good relationships with the customers so it will usually assume the accounts receivable and any service contract liabilities. The buyer will not assume past payroll obligations, deferred compensation or professional fees. Sometimes the assumption of liabilities can be a significant portion of the transaction value.

SALE OF STOCK

The purchase of stock is a fairly straightforward transaction structure. However, a purchase of stock is riskier for the buyer than a purchase of assets. The reason is that there may be the possibility of unknown liabilities. To make sure that there are no unknown liabilities, the due diligence process can be much more complicated and protracted. The buyer wants to make absolutely sure that there are not any liabilities that might surface down the road.

FORMS OF PAYMENT

The currency used to pay for the acquisition of a company includes cash, stock, notes or a combination of these. The buyer may assume liabilities or make future payments based on performance, known as an earnout.

Cash is very straightforward. Sometimes the buyer will request that 10 percent to 15 percent of the purchase price be placed in an escrow account for 12 months in case any problems surface after the transaction has closed.

Sellers typically want all cash; however, payment in stock may be advantageous for several reasons. The seller may receive a higher dollar value if paid in stock rather than cash. The buyer's stock may be more liquid and perhaps less risky than the seller's stock that they currently own. The stock of the buyer could become liquid in the near future and the stock might increase in value. In addition, taxes can be deferred until the stock is eventually sold.

If accepting payment in stock, the seller needs to determine if the price of the stock is reasonable. This is true whether the buyer is a publicly traded company or a private company. If private, what valuation is being used to determine the price of the buyer's shares? If a company trades its stock for stock of the buyer, the transaction will be tax free in most situations. If stock is sold for cash, the shareholders will have to pay taxes on the capital gain.

Occasionally, a transaction will be structured in which the buyer pays a portion with a promissory note. These notes typically have a moderate interest rate and are payable over a period of two to five years. Buyers like using promissory notes because they can purchase a company without requiring as much cash up front.

Consulting Contracts and Noncompetes

Many transactions include consulting contracts and noncompete agreements. Consulting contracts are made with key management people to help with the transition period. These contracts typically last from six months to as long as two years.

Noncompete agreements are standard in the sale of companies. By signing a noncompete agreement, an employee agrees not to work for a competitor for a period of time—typically one or two years. The buyer can pay the manager a specified dollar amount for agreeing to the noncompete agreement.

Thomas Metz

23 EARNOUTS

An earnout can be a versatile tool to bridge the price gap between what a seller thinks his company is worth and what the buyer is willing to pay. In other words, they can't agree on price. The parties may have differing views about future profits or the certainty of achieving them.

An earnout is a mechanism in which a portion of the price is contingent upon future performance. A typical earnout might include a down payment plus future payments based on a percentage of revenues or a percentage of operating income that exceeds a certain threshold.

Earnouts are most successful when the operating entity continues to be independent after the acquisition. If not structured properly, earnouts can put a strain on the working relationship between management of the acquired company and the buyer.

Earnouts should not be used when the operations are tightly integrated. It is difficult to determine if the objectives were achieved because of the entrepreneur's efforts or because of the buyer's actions. In the technology markets, operations are often tightly integrated into the buying company which makes earnouts unwieldy.

Generally I am not in favor of earnouts. A simple transaction structure is usually the best transaction structure. Earnouts are often the result of a buyer and a seller who are unwilling to compromise and structures can get unduly complicated.

If you do decide to utilize an earnout, use milestones that are easily measurable—such as revenues, rather than profits.

Graduated payments are better than all or nothing schemes. Make sure that the definitions used are clear and precise. (For example, how are net sales defined?) Management should have the resources and freedom necessary to pursue their objectives. It is important to commit to a budget, especially a marketing budget. Put a limit on the timeframe for the earnout; three years should be the maximum.

24 UNDERSTANDING DUE DILIGENCE

Due diligence is a fundamental part of any sale-of-company transaction. There are numerous misconceptions about this topic. What exactly is due diligence? What does it involve? When does it begin? How long does it last? This chapter presents a brief overview of the due diligence process.

In simple terms, due diligence is the process by which the buyer researches the selling company in more depth and confirms the accuracy of statements made by the seller. The buyer wants to make sure that there are no additional risks or issues that have not been disclosed.

Due diligence usually begins after the letter of intent has been signed. The buyer will send the seller a lengthy list of the items that it wishes to review. The buyer will want to review detailed financial statements and supporting schedules, corporate records, customer information, product information, intellectual property records and so on.

The buyer wants to make sure that there are no hidden or off-balance-sheet liabilities. It must satisfy itself that there are no potential lawsuits and no employee grievances. Occasionally, problems that crop up during due diligence can result in a reduction of purchase price or even a reopening of negotiations.

The process typically lasts from three to seven weeks. It is completed when the buyer is satisfied that it has adequately researched the various aspects of the seller's business. A detailed due diligence list can be as long as 20 pages. A sample due diligence list is presented in Appendix E.

OVERVIEW OF DUE DILIGENCE TOPICS

Let us review some of the various aspects of due diligence.

Financial Statements

The buyer will want to review the financial statements for the last three to five years including the supporting schedules. The current budget and financial projections will be requested as well. A seller that is well prepared will have written explanations for unusual items such as write-downs, prepaid items, deferred items, etc.

Contracts and Agreements

The buyer's team will review all contracts, agreements and licenses. An important question is—can these contracts be assigned to a buyer upon sale of the company? Is there liability for warranty services going forward?

Intellectual Property

A review of the company's intellectual property is an important matter. This includes patents, copyrights, software, trademarks and trade secrets. The ownership of all intellectual property should be well documented. Licensing agreements related to patents should also be disclosed. Ownership and licensing of software is important.

Customers

The buyer will want to review a schedule of revenues by customer. The buyer may request to have telephone conversations with a few key customers, especially those that account for a large portion of the seller's revenues.

Employees

Information on employees includes the organization chart, a list of employees including position, salary and time with the company. Copies of employee agreements, deferred compensation programs and employee benefit plans should be made available for the buyer.

Operations and Facilities

The buyer will have questions about operations. What services do you outsource? What software systems do you employ? Provide a description of all your facilities including real estate and a copy of your building lease.

Corporate Information

The buyer will review all corporate documents including the articles of incorporation, corporate bylaws and so on. The buyer will also want to review the capitalization table and any shareholder agreements and stock option plans. Due diligence also includes potential litigation, environmental matters and tax matters.

An essential aspect of perfecting your exit strategy is to have well-organized corporate information, accurate financial statements, up-to-date intellectual property records and generally good records regarding all aspects of the company. The more information that can be prepared ahead of time, the smoother the due diligence process will be.

Thomas Metz

25 THE PURCHASE AGREEMENT

The purchase agreement is the definitive document that specifies the price and the terms of the transaction as well as the closing date. This agreement is usually drafted by the buyer's attorneys and then reviewed by the seller's attorneys. The all-important section on price usually requires only a paragraph or two to describe.

One important area of the purchase agreement is the section on representations and warranties. These are statements made by both parties on a variety of issues. "Reps and warranties" confirm that the seller has disclosed all the important items to the buyer and that certain items are true.

A representation is a *declaration* about a specific fact. A warranty is an *assurance*. Representations and warranties cover a wide range of areas. The buyer wants to be assured that there are not any unknown risks. Occasionally the reps and warranties can be problematic.

Typical reps and warranties include items like the corporation is duly organized; the board of directors has authorized the agreement; the financial statements are accurate; the company has no off-balance-sheet liabilities; patents and trademarks have been duly registered; there are no pending lawsuits and the tax returns have been filed.

The buyer wants the representations and warranties to be as broad as possible. Typically there are a few exceptions that qualify some reps and warranties and these exceptions are cited in the document. The reps and warranties are usually in effect for a period of two years.

The buyer will also make a few reps and warranties but they are more limited. They affirm that its corporation is duly organized and has the authority to enter into the agreement. The purchaser will state that it will not be in violation of any laws and that it has the financial capacity to consummate the acquisition.

COVENANTS AND OTHER ITEMS

The purchase agreement will also include a number of covenants. A *covenant* is a promise to do something or to not do something from the signing of the agreement until closing or following the closing.

Provisions in the purchase agreement specify that the seller promises to operate its business in its ordinary fashion and the seller will not enter into any new contracts or incur liabilities above a certain dollar amount. The agreement describes how employee matters should be dealt with such as benefit plans and employment offers.

The purchase agreement also includes *indemnifications*. The seller will indemnify the buyer against all claims or losses as a result of any breach of a representation or warranty. For example, if any litigation is pending, the seller might indemnify the buyer against the cost of the litigation.

Escrow is utilized in some transactions. If escrow is used, a portion of the purchase price (typically 10 percent) is held back and put into an escrow account for up to a year. If there are any discrepancies later, the buyer has a mechanism to recover these amounts.

If the buyer is a company with a publicly traded stock, the seller may not immediately sell the shares. The shares may be restricted from trading for a period of time. The purchase document will spell out the details of the registration rights.

The closing of the transaction usually occurs on the same day that the legal documents are signed; however, in some cases the closing may be delayed for a few weeks.

26 TAX PLANNING

Selling a business can involve serious tax consequences. Some issues can become quite complex. It is important to get the advice of an accountant or an attorney who has experience working with sale-of-company transactions.

An important issue is asset allocation. The way that the purchase price is allocated will affect the tax situation. The buyer and seller must agree on how to allocate the purchase price. For example, what portion of the price is allocated for inventory, what portion for patents, etc. The buyer and seller must use the same amounts for each allocation. Generally, what is good for the buyer is bad for the seller and vice versa.

As we discussed in the chapter on transaction structures, if a C Corporation sells its assets, the business pays capital gains tax and the shareholders also pay tax when the money is distributed to them. The gain is the amount that the sale price exceeds the assets' cost basis. Thus, there is double taxation when a C Corporation sells assets. It is better for a C Corporation to sell its shares of stock rather than its assets.

When selling an S Corporation or an LLC, the owner pays personal tax on any gains. S corporations and LLCs do not pay tax at the corporate level.

Start planning early. Understand the tax impact of various transaction structures ahead of time. Sell off assets that are not fundamental to the business such as real estate. If you need to change the status of the corporation, it might take several years to be effective. The next chapter offers advice on how to hire the appropriate tax advisor, accountant and attorney.

Thomas Metz

27 THE RIGHT ATTORNEY AND ACCOUNTANT

Experience is the key to key to hiring the best professionals. An attorney or an accountant with significant experience with the sale of companies will be able to properly address the issues and deal with problems that inevitably arise. The right advisors can make the transaction proceed more smoothly and minimize the chances of difficulties arising down the road.

The accountant's primary responsibility is the preparation and review of your financial statements. These statements must be accurate and up-to-date. The accountant must also be able to explain any unusual items to the buyer and assist with due diligence information. The accountant can offer structuring advice in order to reduce the tax consequences for the seller.

It may be smart to bring in an outside accounting firm six or nine months prior to the sale to get the company's financial house in order. Financial statements that are accurate and complete give a buyer a strong sense of comfort regarding the company.

The selling company will need an experienced transaction attorney. An attorney who has been through the M&A process multiple times will have the experience and judgment to be an effective adviser.

It is a mistake to use your normal business attorney or your college friend who incorporated the company when you founded it years ago. An experienced transaction attorney may cost a little more, but the expense is well worth it.

The attorney should review the company's contracts and

agreements to ensure that they are accurate, up-to-date and transferable. Other issues to be addressed include employment issues, insurance matters, intellectual property issues, etc. Do not let your attorney negotiate the transaction on your behalf. Occasionally legal issues can become problematic and the attorney may end up attempting to negotiate the transaction terms. Remember, the attorney's job is to offer legal advice to the CEO and board members, not negotiate the transaction. Legal issues should not drive the transaction. The investment banker or an experienced board member is in a much better position to negotiate.

Over the years, I have rescued a number of transactions in which problems arose because the attorneys did not correctly understand the situation and the client's objectives. One of the investment banker's roles is to oversee the various advisers. As an experienced and objective third party, the investment banker can make sure that the accountant and attorney are working with the client's true objectives in mind.

28 USING AN INTERMEDIARY

The assistance of an experienced adviser, such as an investment banker, can be invaluable. As an objective third party, he or she can manage the transaction process and help overcome problems that inevitably crop up. The banker can also play an important role in negotiations. Ensure success by bringing in an intermediary with significant transaction experience. Mistakes can be costly.

Companies usually have three objectives when seeking to sell the business. First of all, they want to get the transaction completed. They want it closed with the best buyer at the best price. In addition they want it closed in a timely manner with a minimum of disruption. The involvement of an experienced investment banker increases the odds that the transaction will be concluded at the best price and with the fewest problems.

The investment banker should be viewed as part of the company's team, as a partner. The banker can contribute his or her experience, judgment and objectivity to the team. The banker should manage the sale process, handle communications with buyers and be the primary point person for negotiations.

Experience is the most important asset that the investment banker brings to the process. The benefit of experience is good judgment and good judgment increases the odds of a successful transaction. The broader an investment banker's experience, the more skilled he or she will be at overcoming the problems, negotiating successfully and getting the deal closed.

The transaction experience that an investment banker brings

113

to the table is different from that of a CEO, venture capitalist or board member. Occasionally, the CEO or a director has been through the sale-of-company process before, sometimes multiple times. They think they understand the sale process extremely well. This can be problematic because human beings have a tendency to over-generalize from small sample sizes. I have experienced this numerous times.

Each sale-of-company transaction is unique. The transaction structures may be similar, but the people and personalities are different. The problems and obstacles are different. The components of value are distinct and different. The negotiating styles are different. Many aspects of the transactions are different.

Every transaction presents unique challenges. The tactics that worked on a previous company sale may not work on this company sale. The investment banker will have been involved in many more transactions. For example, I have been involved in the sale of more than 100 companies. This is significantly more transaction experience than that of the board members or CEO. Why is this important? Because this depth of experience enables me to communicate effectively with the other side and diffuse personality issues. Extensive experience enables me to avoid problem areas, overcome obstacles, devise creative solutions, fine tune the deal structure, get the parties to agree and close the transaction at the best price.

The benefit of experience is particularly important with respect to the nuances and subtleties. How do you know if the other side is telling you their real objectives? Do they mean what they say? Are they bluffing? Can we ask for another $1 million without spoiling the transaction? Should we *demand* another $1 million? Should we ask that question of the CEO or the CFO? And the list goes on. These are gray area questions. And the gray areas are where experience is needed most.

Let me give you an example of how experience plays out. A few years ago I sold a robotics company for $30 million. The founder and his wife were hoping to get $12 to $15 million. After participating in a number of meetings and phone calls with the buyer, it became very clear to me that the seller's technology would give the buyer a distinct competitive advantage. The negotiations were friendly and professional. I asked a variety of probing questions over a period of weeks to confirm my instinct that the technology was highly strategic to the buyer. The transaction successfully closed and both parties were happy.

Of course, I am not going to achieve such dramatic results every time. My experience urged me to continue to ask probing questions and to listen diligently. In this case, I was effective at reading the other side, understanding their true needs and figuring out a solution that both parties were happy with. Negotiating is the most important role that the investment banker can perform.

Objectivity is an advantage that the investment banker brings to the process as well. The intermediary can help a company owner perceive the business through the eyes of a buyer. An interesting dynamic is one I call the "third-party dynamic." A buyer may mention something to me in passing that he would never say directly to the seller. These are not major revelations, but the information can be useful in reaching compromises or overcoming problems.

The tasks that an investment banker or intermediary performs include:

- Manage the sale process
- Identify potential buyers
- Overcome obstacles and solve problems
- Negotiate with buyers
- Drive the deal forward
- Maintain confidentiality
- Ensure that the transaction gets closed

Let us examine each of these topics in more detail.

Manage the Sale Process

Managing the overall sale process is the essential activity that the investment banker performs. This includes getting buyers to the table at the same time, negotiating the price and terms and making sure that the transaction closes.

Sometimes a CEO will decide to manage the sale process and sell his or her own company. The task of selling a company is a full-time endeavor; there are no shortcuts. The transaction will be shortchanged if a CEO tries to run the company and manage the process at the same time. The CEO can add the most value by running the company, keeping customers satisfied, managing employees, increasing revenues and building value. Appendix D discusses the myth about CEOs selling their own companies.

Identify Potential Buyers

Identifying potential buyers is a fairly straightforward task. Viewing the market sectors from a fresh perspective is an advantage that the investment banker can bring to the process. Most bankers are quite resourceful in reaching out to adjacent markets to identify buyers beyond the obvious candidates.

Sometimes a management team will have preconceived ideas about who the best buyers are. They may have issues with some potential buyers in the market for various reasons. The set of good buyers can shift quickly; a firm that was not a good buyer three years ago may be an excellent buyer now. As an objective third party, the investment banker can set aside any preconceived notions.

Problem Solving

Every transaction will encounter obstacles and problems, usually multiple problems. A banker who has been down these roads before will have the experience to overcome the obstacles. He will know how to deal with personalities, head off small issues before they become serious and keep the parties on track.

Getting a transaction unstuck is one of the most important tasks that an investment banker can perform. Almost half of all transactions fall apart at least once. An experienced banker can get a transaction back on track once it has become derailed.

Negotiating

An objective third party can be more effective in negotiations. An intermediary can establish a constructive atmosphere, help defuse unreasonable claims and minimize extreme posturing. He or she can gauge reactions and devise compromises.

As a professional negotiator, one of the most important things that I have learned is to understand precisely where the other side is coming from and what their true objectives are.

In many cases the buyer will have previously made acquisitions; thus, its team has experience in negotiating the purchase of a company. The same is generally not true for sellers; most have not sold a company before. It pays to have an experienced negotiator in your corner.

Drive the Deal Forward

Sometimes the banker needs to be somewhat aggressive in driving the transaction forward. If the CEO is pushing the transaction hard, it can suggest to the buyer that the selling company is desperate. An intermediary can drive the transaction without the seller appearing desperate or too anxious to sell.

Maintain Confidentiality

Maintaining confidentiality can be an essential aspect for the sale of some companies. As a third party, the investment banker can effectively manage and maintain confidentiality throughout the transaction process.

Get the Transaction Closed

The greatest value that an investment banker adds is getting the parties to agree and actually getting the transaction closed. This is where the investment banker really earns his or her fee.

HOW MUCH ARE THE FEES?

The investment banker is paid for results, i.e., for getting a transaction closed. This success fee is usually a percentage of the transaction value. Most investment bankers charge a retainer, paid up front or monthly. The retainer obligates the banker to the transaction and it demonstrates commitment on the part of the selling company. Without a retainer, there is an incentive for the banker to go after the low hanging fruit and not go the extra mile. The client is not well served in this case. In addition, an exclusive agreement gives the banker an incentive to put in a significant effort for the client.

The size of the fee depends on the size of transaction. Large transactions pay a small percentage. Over $50 million or $100 million the fee might be 2% or 3% of the transaction value. For transactions from $10 million to $50 million the fee ranges from about 3% to 6%. For transactions between $2 million and $10 million the fee might range from 5% to 8%. Below $2 million, the fee might be 10% or 12%.

Make sure that the investment banker's fee is tightly aligned with the shareholders' objectives. Most sellers confirm that the value that the banker adds is well worth the fee.

Appendix C offers some advice on how to select an investment banker. For a more detailed discussion on investment banking fees and fee agreements, refer to *Selling the Intangible Company.*

AFTERWORD

Hopefully the book will have achieved its objective which is to help entrepreneurs and company owners sell their companies at the most attractive price and with the fewest problems along the way.

Good things happen when companies are prepared. Many entrepreneurs and CEOs are so busy running the company that they don't have time to stop and think about some of the ideas that I discuss in the book. It is my hope that I have opened their eyes to some issues that they can address so that when the time comes to sell, the process will be smooth sailing and the price will be very attractive.

If you are interested in learning more about the topics in this book, you may wish to read the more in-depth book. It is entitled *Selling the Intangible Company—How to Negotiate and Capture the Value of a Growth Firm*. This book includes 50 actual examples, or "war stories," that illustrate many of the topics. Please see www.intangiblecompany.com for more information.

ACKNOWLEDGEMENTS

I would like to thank a number of people for their help and sharing ideas for this book. A special thanks to Phil Herres who patiently gave me his feedback and insights. I value his opinions. I would like to acknowledge Karen Mooney for her input and valuable suggestions. Thanks to Ed Garth, Doug Seto, and Diana Woodin for their ideas and critiques. I would also like to thank Mitchell Hymowitz, Chris Dishman, John Atherly, and Samantha Woogerd. Thanks to Bob Farrell for his contributions and for the summer sail. For his visual talents with the cover art, I would like to thank my brother Peter Metz of Sockeye.

Appendices

APPENDIX A: TRADITIONAL VALUATION METHODS

This appendix briefly explains the three traditional valuation methods. Each of these methods determines value from a different angle. Understanding these valuation methods is useful, not because they correctly value a company, but because they may arise in negotiations. This section is not intended to give the reader an in-depth understanding of valuation methods, but to provide an overview of the three fundamental approaches to valuation. The traditional methods for determining value include:

- Market Approach
- Asset Approach
- Income Approach

THE MARKET APPROACH

The Market Approach is generally the best method to value a company. The Market Approach calculates value by comparing the firm to other companies in the industry, typically using multiples of earnings.

The difficulty is finding companies that are truly comparable. It is also difficult to find information about comparable transactions that are private. In fast-moving industries, such as technology and software, few companies are similar enough for comparisons to be valid.

For a publicly traded company the firm's value is calculated by the price of the company's stock. The Price Earnings (P/E) ratio is the stock price divided by the earnings per share. Stock prices have averaged 15 times earnings over the last 80 years for publicly traded companies. High growth companies have price earnings ratios greater than that and low growth companies have price earnings ratios less than that.

For privately held companies the most widely used metric for calculating value is the multiple of operating profits. Operating profits are defined as earnings before interest, taxes, depreciation and amortization, or EBITDA. This basically measures a company's cash flow. Private equity firms often use the valuation metric of five or six times EBITDA to determine the value of a company.

THE ASSET APPROACH

The Asset Approach involves calculating the market value of each of the company's assets: accounts receivable, inventory, equipment, buildings, and so on. The market value for these assets is usually the replacement cost. This valuation method is rarely applicable to technology companies because most technology and software firms have few tangible assets.

The primary asset of a technology or software company is its intellectual property. It is extremely difficult to place a value on intellectual property. Even though it may have required many man-years to develop, the value depends on what a buyer is willing to pay for it.

THE INCOME APPROACH

The Income Approach utilizes discounted future cash flows. This is also called net present value. The concept is that dollars received in future years are not as valuable as dollars received this year.

A company's projected cash flows are discounted at a percentage known as the discount rate. This rate is a measure of the uncertainty about achieving the projected earnings. Put another way, the discount rate is the return that investors expect given the amount of risk. Risky companies have higher discount rates and less risky companies have lower rates.

The required return to investors for a company with less than about $20 million in revenue will usually be from 20 percent to 25 percent. The required return will be higher if the company has a limited history or significant business risk. The discount rate is calculated by adding the premiums for various types of risk. The starting point is the risk-free rate on 20 year treasury bonds. A risk premium is added for each risk—equity risk, size risk and company specific risk. Stocks are riskier than government bonds, so add 8%. Small companies are riskier than large companies, thus the size premium. Company specific risk accounts for factors such as technology risk, market risk, financial risk, etc. Below is an example of the discount rate calculation:

Risk-free rate (20-year T-bonds)	2.5%
Equity risk premium	8.0%
Size risk premium	5.0%
Company specific risk	6.0%
Total discount rate	21.5%

An illustration of the discounted cash flow calculation is shown in Table A-1 below. Note that the cash flow is after taxes. In this example the company has cash flows of $1.4 million in the first year, $1.6 million in the second year, and so on. The terminal value assumes that the cash flow from year five will continue indefinitely. The terminal value is calculated by dividing the year five cash flow by the discount rate.

Table A-1: Example of Discounted Cash Flow Calculation

($ millions)	Year 1	Year 2	Year 3	Year 4	Year 5	Terminal Value
Cash Flow	1.4	1.6	1.8	2.0	2.3	10.5
Discount Rate	22%					
Net Present Value	$8.1					

The drawback of this method is that revenues and profits are projections and the assumptions are subjective. Optimistic projections can result in a value that may not be realistic. This model only makes sense is if the projections are reasonable and based on sound assumptions.

Thomas Metz

APPENDIX B: EIGHT M&A MYTHS

Myths are the so-called truths that many people believe about the sale-of-company process. Myths perpetuate because people do not question established views. In this appendix we debunk eight myths regarding the sale of companies:

1. The Myth of Intrinsic Value
2. The Myth of a Narrow Value Range
3. The Myth of Revenue Multiples
4. The Myth of Liquidity
5. The Myth of Big Buyers
6. The Myth that Small M&A is like Big M&A
7. The Myth that the CEO Should Sell the Company
8. The Rolodex Myth

THE MYTH OF INTRINSIC VALUE

The myth is that the value of a company is intrinsic. The reality is that the value of the company is extrinsic.

Simply put, the value of your company is what a buyer will pay you for it. Value exists only in the context of the marketplace. The real issue here is not about intrinsic or extrinsic value but about the nature of markets. When the market is deep, with many buyers and sellers, it is easy to determine the price for a good or service (intrinsic value). When the market is thin, with only a few buyers and sellers, it is difficult to determine an accurate value.

Companies with strategic value have a limited number of

potential buyers. The reason is because their unique technology is of high strategic interest to only a few buyers. Remember that strategic value is always greater than financial value.

For companies with financial value there are many buyers, particularly private equity groups (if the transaction is large enough). There may be several hundred potential buyers for a financial acquisition. These buyers will pay a price that falls in a narrow range of value.

With only a few legitimate buyers for a strategic sale, a true market does not exist, thus there is no market price and no intrinsic value. Value is a function of how much a buyer is willing to pay.

THE MYTH OF A NARROW VALUE RANGE

The myth is that value falls within a narrow range. The reality is that a company's value can vary dramatically when the value is strategic.

In the markets that most people are most familiar with, houses and cars, value falls within a narrow range. The value of your house may range from $575,000 to $675,000. The high value is about 17% greater than the low value.

The value of a company whose value is strategic may range from $3 million to $8 million. The high value is more than twice the low value. The difference in these values represents the difference in the strategic importance to buyers. Thus, the value range is wide, not narrow.

THE MYTH OF REVENUE MULTIPLES

The myth is that a multiple of revenues is a good way to value a company. The reality is that this is a poor measure of value.

Multiples of revenue do not take into consideration profitability, expenses, market position or growth. These matters are important valuation characteristics of any business. A slowly growing company is not worth as much as a rapidly growing company; a highly profitable company is worth more than a barely profitable company—even if their revenues are the same.

Secondly, the range of values is so wide to be of little use. Multiples of revenue typically range between .4 times and 4.0 times.

A company with $2 million in revenues is worth between $800,000 and $8 million. This is such a wide range that it is of no help at all.

Thirdly, a multiple from one transaction is rarely comparable to other transactions. Just because one company sold for 2 times its revenues does not mean that another company will sell for 2 times their revenues. The reason is that these are unique transactions; they are not comparable from one to another. The value of strategic assets is unrelated to the revenue stream. The revenues could be half or double and the key asset is still the same.

Buyers may *talk* in terms of revenue multiples, but buyers do not *think* in such terms. Buyers think in terms of how much value they can create with a particular acquisition. How will the acquisition speed market entry? What additional operating profits will it generate? The revenue multiple is not relevant. Sometimes revenue multiples are interjected as a negotiating ploy. A buyer may cite some revenue multiples to make their offer appear attractive, but it is simply not germane.

THE MYTH OF LIQUIDITY

The myth is that when a company sells, the shareholders always achieve liquidity. The reality is that the shareholders may not get cashed out.

The selling shareholders are not always cashed out. Sometimes they receive stock of the acquiring company and sometimes the transaction is structured as an earnout. The reason that they might accept stock is because they prefer the buyer's stock to their own stock; the acquiring company is likely a larger and less risky company.

The management team of the selling company often stays on board for a period of time, typically six months to a year. So they cannot purchase a sailboat and cruise around the world just yet. If the transaction includes an earnout, the team will have strong incentives to stay on board and continue building the company.

THE MYTH OF BIG BUYERS

The myth is that the big companies are the best buyers. The reality is that midsized and smaller companies are usually the best buyers.

For a large transaction, say more than $100 million, a large buyer is a given. Sometimes large buyers (with more than $500 million in revenues) will acquire companies in the $30 million to $75 million range, but these are exceptions. The best buyer for a transaction in this size range is a midsized company, with revenues from $50 million to $250 million.

For small transactions, less than $30 million, the best buyers are midsized buyers and smaller buyers. The acquisition of an $8 million company is immaterial to a $1 billion company but it could be quite meaningful to a $35 million revenue company.

Ego can come into play here. An entrepreneur would rather tell her friends that she sold to Google or Amazon than to some lesser known company.

THE MYTH THAT SMALL M&A IS LIKE BIG M&A

The myth is that the sale process for small transactions is the same as that for large transactions. The reality is that the process for selling a smaller company is different.

Many people assume that the process for selling a small company is the same as that for selling a large company. Large transactions are generally conducted with the two-step auction process that we discussed in Chapter 18. This process is effective at closing transactions in a reasonable time frame and for a good price. The auction method works well for companies whose value is financial, not strategic.

On the other hand, a negotiated sale is the best method for selling smaller companies and those with strategic value. In addition, companies whose value is strategic have a much smaller universe of buyers that companies with financial value.

THE MYTH THAT THE CEO SHOULD SELL THE COMPANY

The myth is that many CEOs think that they should sell their own companies. The reality is that the CEO should never sell his or her own company.

At first this seems reasonable. After all, the CEO knows her business, she knows the market and she knows how to negotiate. The first problem is that a CEO is simply not objective. In addition, perceptive listening is a key negotiating skill; CEOs are not usually the best listeners.

Secondly, selling a company is a very time consuming process. There is no way that a CEO can manage the sale process and run the company at the same time. Either the process will be shortchanged or the company will not be managed effectively.

When a CEO sells his own company he typically contacts only a small set of buyers. He does not have the time to reach out to a large number. He convinces himself that he knows the market well and therefore knows the best buyers. He rarely contacts nonobvious buyers in adjacent markets. In these cases, the shareholders are not well served.

THE ROLODEX MYTH

The myth is that contacts and relationships are the key to finding the right buyer. The reality is that contacts are the easy part; getting the transaction closed is the difficult part.

Many people think that contacts, relationships and "knowing a space" is the key to successfully selling a company. The New York investment banks are organized around industry lines. However, in markets where value is strategic, like the technology and software industries, the markets are like the Wild West—the landscape is rapidly changing. New companies pop up all the time, some firms are acquired, some experience rapid growth and some go out of business. The people are continually changing jobs as well. Six months is a very long time in the technology business.

A primary skill of investment bankers is knowing how to drill down on an industry. Making contacts is not a problem since most companies are open to considering acquisitions. Certainly contacts and relationships do not hurt, but the crucial skill that an investment banker brings to the process is the ability to get a transaction closed.

Thomas Metz

APPENDIX C: SELECTING AN INVESTMENT BANKER

This section is intended to help CEOs and boards of directors make the best decision when hiring an investment banker for the sale of a company.

Transaction experience is the key competency that an investment banker brings to the party. The deeper an investment banker's experience, the better his or her judgment and the more skilled he will be at overcoming problems and effectively closing the transaction.

Experience covers a number of areas: experience running the sale process, experience dealing with many buyers and sellers, experience overcoming obstacles and, of course, experience in negotiations. The broader the base of experience the more effective the banker will be at completing a transaction successfully.

Three criteria are essential for selecting an investment banker—competence, character and commitment. Let us review these criteria.

COMPETENCE

Competence is the ability to get a deal done at the best price and in a timely manner. Competence is highly correlated with experience. The banker with the most experience will likely have the greatest set of skills for solving the transaction issues and adopting the appropriate negotiation posture. It also includes the unique competency known as deal savvy.

Imagination and creativity are qualities that separate the good dealmakers from the great dealmakers. Difficult problems require imaginative solutions. A creative dealmaker reframes problems, gets outside the box and devises new solutions. Every transaction will have difficulties and the experienced deal maker anticipates problems and negotiates a successful outcome. Effective negotiators have excellent people skills and good communication skills.

Choose an investment banker that has experience on transactions that are similar in size to your transaction. For transactions greater than $150 million, a big New York investment bank is a good choice. Between $30 million and $150 million, a midsized investment bank is the best fit. For transactions less than $30 million, select a boutique firm. A small firm is more likely to provide full attention on these smaller transactions.

Deal savvy is an elusive quality. Deal savvy means simply knowing how to make deals happen. Deal savvy enables the investment banker to deal with bluffs, false objections and other obstacles. He knows where there is weakness and where there is strength. In the end, a banker with deal savvy will find a way to get the transaction closed.

CHARACTER

Character embodies trust, integrity and chemistry. The banker should have integrity with respect to the client. This means communicating issues honestly and truthfully, including bad news.

Integrity in negotiating means building trust with both sides. Shifting positions does not generate trust. Integrity also means staying true to your word.

Management should enjoy and respect the professional with whom they are working. Good chemistry is a strong foundation for discussions in case problems arise. The principals of a company will be spending a good six months with the advisor so choose wisely.

COMMITMENT

Committed attention is the most important thing that an investment banker can provide to his or her client. Is the transaction large enough to get the banker's interest? Who is the person that will be working on your transaction? Is it a senior partner or a junior person? Will the banker give fully committed attention to the transaction and to the client?

Commitment is important because transactions always have issues. When the going gets tough will the investment banker move on to the next deal or will he stay committed and find a way to get the transaction closed?

Thomas Metz

APPENDIX D: OPTIMUM PRICE AND MARKET TIMING

Market timing has more influence on price than any other factor when selling a company. Paying attention to the reality of the market is the primary requisite for realizing the optimum price.

The biggest exit mistake companies make is that they decide to sell too late in the game. If a company waits to sell until its revenues have peaked, there may be little growth left. The problem is that this timing is often unrelated to the market situation. The highest value is achieved by capitalizing on the right market condition.

THE MARKET LIFE CYCLE

The life cycle of a market consists of five stages—early development, growth, maturity, decline and consolidation. We have all seen graphs depicting these stages. The same graph illustrates the optimal time to sell.

In the early development stage, several small companies are developing technologies and scrambling to get customers. There are few, if any, medium-sized companies because the market is new.

In the growth stage, these small firms experience increasing revenues. These firms do not want to be acquired at this stage because they are growing nicely. Sometimes a less successful company will be acquired because it is having difficulty getting market traction. Ironically, this second-tier player now has access to greater sales resources and could subsequently become a strong force in the market.

Large companies rarely move early into new markets. They want to enter big markets, so they wait until they are sure that the market is significant. When the first big company enters the market, this is designated as the *pre-turning point*. A graphical depiction of selling price versus market stage in shown in Figure D-1 below.

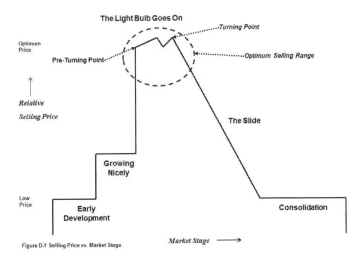

Figure D-1 Selling Price vs. Market Stage

THE LIGHT BULB GOES ON

The next stage, the *lightbulb* stage, is when a few more large firms decide to enter the market. Acquisitions are a good way for these companies to establish a foothold in a new market. Rarely will there be more than three or four big players entering a young market.

The lesson is that if a company wants to sell, the perfect time is when one of the big companies wants to enter the market. The first company to sell often obtains the best price because it has the first seller advantage. When no more big companies are entering the market, this means the turning point is at hand.

THE SLIDE

The *slide* begins after the large players have moved in. In this phase the big companies are grabbing market share and perhaps entering foreign markets. It is difficult for the smaller players to compete with these large companies.

CONSOLIDATION

In the *consolidation* phase the only reason for a large company to make an acquisition is to add customers. The large companies already have their own technology; they don't need to acquire to gain technology. The price of an acquisition is not particularly high when the primary asset is the customer base.

In summary, if a company wants to sell for the optimum price, it must pay attention to the stage of the market. This goes against the instincts of many entrepreneurs who tend to focus on their own technologies, products and growth. The state of the market is the primary driver for realizing the optimum price in the sale of a company.

Thomas Metz

APPENDIX E: DUE DILIGENCE CHECKLIST

This is an example of a due diligence checklist. The list is fairly comprehensive even though this list is actually abbreviated from the original version. Some items may not apply to your situation; however, the list will give you a good perspective of what is involved in the due diligence process.

Financial Statements

1. Historical financial statements for the last four years (balance sheet, income statement, cash flow statement)
2. Budget for the current year
3. Income statement forecast for the next two or three years
4. Describe your policy for revenue recognition
5. Describe other significant accounting policies (e.g., depreciation)
6. List all deferred income items
7. List all deferred expenses and liabilities
8. Aged accounts receivable report and bad debt report
9. Describe any accounting changes or conventions
10. Documents and letters from auditors regarding their information requests
11. Document any off-balance-sheet liabilities and commitments

Corporate Documents

1. Articles of incorporation and bylaws
2. Corporate minute books and resolutions

3. Reports to shareholders
4. Capitalization table
5. List of all shareholders
6. Agreements regarding voting rights
7. Agreements regarding registration rights or first right of refusal
8. Compensation table
9. Stock option plans

Tax Documents

1. Copies of all tax returns (federal, state and local) for the last three years
2. List any pending issues regarding tax matters
3. List any tax liens and unresolved issues with the IRS or other tax authorities

Management and Employees

Management Information
1. Organization chart
2. Management biographies
3. List of company directors and background information
4. Insurance policies for directors and officers
5. Company stock option and bonus plans
6. Employee benefit plans, insurance plans and medical plans
7. Copy of employee handbook if available
8. Copies of all employment agreements

Employee Information
9. Job descriptions for the various positions
10. Copies of all employment agreements and consulting agreements.
11. List of all employees by functional area

Outside Contractors
12. Copies of agreements with all contractors
13. Copies of agreements with other outside parties
14. Copies of agreements with all software developers

showing that the company is the owner of the IP

General Agreements and Contracts

1. Copies of all current contracts, agreements and commitments
2. List of contracts that will expire in the next year
3. Copies of all agreements with customers, suppliers and distributors
4. Copies of all product warranties and guarantees
5. Copies of all partnering agreements

Market and Product Information

1. Marketing plan by product line
2. Marketing budget for the next few years

Product Information

1. Sales volume for each product in dollars
2. Sales volume for each product in units
3. Profit margin per product
4. Price list for each product
5. Compare your pricing to competitors' pricing
6. Warranty policy and outstanding warranty liabilities

Customer Information

7. List top 15 customers and their revenues
8. List top 15 customers and their profitability
9. List major customers brought in over the last 3 years

Competitor Information

10. List your top five competitors
11. Show approximate market share for each
12. Show competitive matrix if appropriate
13. Describe how you compete against each competitor

Intellectual Property

1. Schedule of all patents and applications
2. List of trademarks and service marks

3. Documents regarding trade secrets and their protection
4. Technology licensing agreements

Other Technology Issues
5. System architecture information
6. Full documentation for software programs
7. Performance metrics for system performance

Legal & Environmental Items

Legal Issues
1. Copies of all documents showing compliance with regulations
2. Describe any existing legal actions
3. Describe any threatened or pending legal actions
4. Documentation and letters relating to any ongoing litigation
5. Documentation and letters relating to infringement of patents or other intellectual property rights
6. Describe any outstanding judgments

Environmental Issues
7. Documents and descriptions of any environmental matters
8. Letters and applications to the EPA or state and local regulatory agencies
9. Copies of complaints and notices from the EPA or other agencies
10. Records of compliance with environmental standards and waste disposal
11. Any other documents regarding environmental issues

ABOUT THE AUTHOR

Thomas V. Metz, Jr. founded the boutique investment bank T.V. Metz & Co., LLC in 1983 and has been an investment banker for more than 30 years. He has a diverse background in corporate finance.

His primary focus is arranging the sale of companies in which the value is strategic, typically in the technology, software and service industries. Mr. Metz has closed transactions across North America as well as Europe and Asia. He has been engaged as a negotiator for sale-of-company transactions and other challenging negotiations.

Earlier in his career he invested venture capital for a private holding company. He held positions in finance with the DeLorean Motor Company and in computer sales with IBM.

Mr. Metz has a Bachelor of Science degree in Mathematics and Computer Science from the University of Oregon. He holds an MBA degree from the University of California at Berkeley. He is a frequent speaker on mergers, acquisitions and entrepreneurial topics. He authored the book *Selling the Intangible Company—How to Negotiate and Capture the Value of a Growth Firm*, published by John Wiley & Sons in 2009.

He is an avid golfer and heli-skier. In his younger years he was a nationally ranked squash player. He is also pilots his airplane, a Cessna 182, to family and golf destinations.

Thomas Metz

INDEX

A

accountants, 111
accounts payable, 49, 98
accounts receivable, 49, 98
acquirers, *See* buyers
adjacent markets, 59
advisor, 93, 111
agreements, *See* contracts and
      agreements
alignment, 5, 36, 78
alternatives, 6, 65, 93
asset approach, 122
asset sale, 97-98
      double taxation and, 98
attorneys, 86, 107, 112
auction method, 87, 128
audit, 40

B

balance sheet, 38, 50
binding paragraphs, 95-96
board of directors, 78, 79, 107,
      112, 131
boutique investment banker, *See*
      investment banker
business:
      definition of, 31, 33, 35
buyers, 20-22, 64
      best, 29
      contacting, 85
      myth of big, 127
      nonobvious, 59

      problems, 28, 72
      sizes of, 26-27, 59-61, 127
      strategic, 21, 25-26, 29, 57

C

capital,
      access to, 6, 9, 28

capital expenditures, 55
capital structure, 31, 37, 69
cash,
      as payment type, 99
cash flow, 14, 54, 122
      multiple, 14
      projection, 39, 123
CEO:
      issues, 42,
      not wanting to sell, 68, 77
      and selling the company, 8,
          128-129
chief executive officer, *See* CEO
closing, 86, 108
competitive bidding, 79
competitors, 34, 49
      as buyers, 28
confidentiality, 85, 89-90, 117
confidentiality agreement, *See*
      NDA
consolidation, 137
consulting agreements, 99
contacts, 3, 43, 44, 48, 71
covenants, 43, 108
CPA, *See* Certified Public
      Accountant
cross-selling opportunities, 16,
      20, 21
customer base, 49, 60, 137
customers, 34
      communicating with, 89
      risks, 53

D

DCF, *See* discounted cash flow
definition,
      of company, 35
descriptive memorandum, *See*
      memorandum

discount rate, 123
discounted cash flow, 122
    example, 123
documents:
    corporate, 44, 105
due diligence, 46, 103-105
    checklist, 139-142

E
earnings before interest, taxes,
    depreciation and
    amortization (EBITDA), 14,
    122
    multiple of, 16, 21
earnouts, 101-102
emerging buyers, 26
employees,
    as buyers, 29
    communicating with, 90
employment agreements, 43
environmental issues, 72
equity risk premium, 123
escrow, 99, 108
exit strategy, 1, 5, 78
    benefits of 5
expectations, 76, 81
experience, 109, 111, 112-116
extended response, 65-66
extrinsic value, 125

F
fair market value
    definition, 16
family businesses, 8
fees,
    agreements, 117
    of investment bankers, 117-
    118
financial:
    buyer, 25
    forecast, 68
    statements, 31, 38-39
    transactions, 13
    value, 14, 21

first seller advantage, 137
forecast, *See* financial forecasts
founders, 8, 39, 44, 51, 69, 73,
    98, 114

G
Gaard Automation, 15
growing nicely stage, 136

I
income approach, *See*
    discounted cash flow
indemnification, 108
intellectual property (IP), 19,
    45-46
    licensing, 70, 72, 82
intermediary, *See* investment
    banker
intrinsic value, 125-126
inventory, 38, 48-49, 71, 97
investment banker, 78, 113-118
    benefits of hiring, 79, 113
    boutique, 132, 143
    fees, 117
    midsized, 132
    role of, 93, 115-117
    selecting, 113, 131-133

K
key customers, 71,0104
key employees, 42, 43, 54, 90

L
lawsuits, 44, 103, 107
leases, 44, 71-72
legal issues, 41, 44, 72, 96, 112
letter of intent (LOI), 86, 95-96
    purpose, 86, 95
liabilities, 50
    assuming, 50, 98
    off balance sheet, 38, 68
    hidden, 38, 67, 68, 103
license agreements, 46, 70, 72,
    104

lightbulb goes on stage, 136
liquidity, 8, 10, 69, 81, 127
liquidation preference, 69
litigation, 50, 67, 72, 105
LOI, *See* letter of intent

M
maintenance revenue, 47-48
management,
  team, 2, 8, 31, 36, 41-42
  risk, 53
market: 34
  approach, 121-122
  entry, 19, 127
  maps, 59
  movement, 57-58
  risk, 53
  timing, 9, 10, 58, 78, 135
  traction, 9, 52, 64, 136
  value, 16, 122
McAfee Associates, 73
measured response, 65
memorandum, 65, 83, 85
mistakes, 27, 75-80, 92
multiple of revenue, 14-16, 76
  myth of, 126
municipal government software,
  58
myths, 125-129

N
NDA, *See* nondisclosure
  agreement
negotiated sale, 87, 128
negotiations, 86, 91-93, 116
  mistakes, 76, 79
  strategies, 91-92
net present value (NPV) *See*
  discounted cash flow
no-hire provision, 95
noncompete agreement, 43, 99
nondisclosure agreement
  (NDA), 85, 89
no-shop clause, 95

O
objectivity, 113, 115
obstacles, 5, 66, 79, 82, 90, 114-
  116, 131
off-balance-sheet, 50, 55, 68,
  103, 107
operating income, 101
operations, 5, 41, 45, 80, 101,
  105
optimum price, 10, 135-137

P
partners, 9, 91
  as buyers, 25, 28
polarized markets, 59-61, 81-82
pre-closing period, 86
pre-turning point, 136
price, *See* purchase price
price-earnings ratio, 122
private companies:
  as buyers, 99
private equity firms, 25-26, 122,
  126
problem solving, 75, 79, 92,
  116, 131
problems, 51, 67, 81
  buyers, 72
  customer, 71
  financial, 67
  intellectual property, 70
  people, 42
  product, 70
  shareholder, 69
process, *See* sale process
profitability, 48
projections, 39
purchase agreement, 107-108
purchase price, 75, 81
  allocation, 109
  range, 16, 92, 126
  setting, 84, 92

R

rapid response, 65
recurring revenue, 47
red flags, 31, 45, 52
representations and warranties,
    107-108
required return on capital, 123
retainers, 117
revenue multiples, *See* multiple
    of revenue
risk,
    business, 32, 123
    recognizing, 22
    reducing, 9, 32, 51-55
risk-free rate, 123
risk premium, 123
rolodex myth, 129

S

sale process, 83-88
    managing the, 87, 89
sales pipeline, 80, 86
shareholder:
    agreement, 105
    issues, 69
    motives, 7
shareholders, 36, 81
    common, 69
    vote, 69
size risk premium, 123
slide stage, 137
small M&A, 128
software as a service, 48
stand-alone company, 22
stay-put bonus, 43
stock,
    buyer's 60, 96, 97, 99
    as consideration, 99
    transaction, 98
strategic value, 13, 15-16, 21, 76,
    77, 87, 88, 91, 125
structure, 97-99, 109
structuring the transaction, 40,
    69, 79, 86, 97-99, 101, 114

synergy, 16

T

tax issues, 39
tax planning, 109
technology, 15, 16, 21, 28, 52,
    70, 81-82, 122
    issues, 70
    selling only, 46
terminal value, 123
third-party dynamic, 115
timing, 10, 58, 78, 82, 135
turning point, 137
total cost of acquisition, 21-22
two-step auction, *See* auction
    method

U

unsolicited offer, 32, 63-66, 80

V

valuation, 76
    methods, 121-123
    professional, 16
value,
    concept of, 75
    improving, 47-50
    range, 126

W

warranties, 107
weaknesses, 32, 51-52
website, 44
working capital, 39, 49-50

54317555R00089

Made in the USA
Charleston, SC
29 March 2016